Praise for *Letting Go, Finding You*

"Hunter Mobley reclaims the Enneagram's original purpose as a tool for transformation, inviting readers into a contemplative journey that frees us from the constraints of conditioned habits. Through soulful honesty and wisdom, Mobley reveals how the Enneagram of Virtues can guide us toward a truly expansive, authentic life."

—**Seth Abrams**, cohost of *Fathoms* Enneagram podcast

"*Letting Go, Finding You* is a tenacious invitation to encounter God and practice a spirituality rooted in goodness and blessing. By connecting Enneagram wisdom with contemplative living, Hunter Mobley opens a door to a kind labyrinth-journey of healing for anyone with the desire to encounter our God-given virtue."

—**D. T. Bryant**, author of *Unless a Seed Falls to the Ground: Welcoming the Death of the Whiteness Gospel* and spiritual director at The Nashville Center for Hope and Healing

"Hunter Mobley is a wisdom friend and teacher for the spiritual journey. In *Letting Go, Finding You* he is a vulnerable, wise, truth-telling guide for how, through engagement with the Enneagram and contemplative spirituality, we can find our way to our true and authentic self. He does this by extending an invitation to surrender, to let go of the striving to be somebody we are not or less than we truly are. He invites readers to embrace the beautiful divine truth of themselves. This is a must-read for anyone who is on the treadmill of continuous striving and weariness of responding to life in habitual ways. It is a life-giving testimony to the healing power of aligning your life with your true self."

—**Mary Jane Cole**, spiritual director, Sacred Path, Inc.

"Jesus once asked, 'Do you want to be made well?' 'Yes!' would be my immediate answer. The 'well'-ness of Jesus, however, emerges from a sacrifice of love. Using the Enneagram, Hunter Mobley provides a spiritually rigorous and transformative pathway that seeks to free us from that which limits our ability to love, to be loved, and consequently to be made well in our relationship with God, ourselves, and our neighbors."

—**Rev. Dr. Donovan Drake**, Westminster Presbyterian Church, Nashville, TN

"Hunter Mobley's engaging personality and teaching style shine in *Letting Go, Finding You*. I have benefited firsthand from his leadership as both a participant in one of his cohorts and as he has led workshops for the congregation I serve as pastor. Are you eager for resources aimed at nurturing a freer, more authentic you? *Letting Go, Finding You* combines Mobley's experience and expertise with the Enneagram and contemplative practice to offer the reader a way into what he is so obviously experiencing in his own life story: authentic, transformative growth."

—**Rev. Dr. Jason Edwards**, senior pastor, Second Baptist Church, Liberty, MO

"Hunter Mobley is an up-and-coming voice in the world of Enneagram reflection and the contemplative path. For people of faith and those who love to dance along the edge of doubt, there is wisdom and courage in this text. Whether you are dipping your toe into the types or you have been plunged beneath the flood for decades, there is healing and hope in this book. Mobley's unique focus on the virtues and not just the vices smacks of a survivor of dualistic religion who embodies our sacred belief in God's sacred image imprinted equally on humanity. Mobley's perspective and exploration of the nine virtues balanced with the nine vices illustrate how we are a blessed blend of light and shadow. As a writer and as a guest lecturer,

Hunter Mobley brings a perspective on the Enneagram that is truly a joy to study."

—**Rev. Dr. Kevin R. Gardner-Sinclair**, pastor, Broadway Baptist Church, Louisville, KY

"The journey inward is the single most important decision a seeker makes when desiring to go deeper with God and others. I need to know I can trust the writer if I'm going to implement their wisdom in daily life. There are very few people I trust more than Hunter Mobley. His mind is sharp, his heart is large, and his soul is good. Mobley has lived out this journey with a fierce love for all people. If, when reading, you get the sense that he has the mind of a lawyer and the heart of a pastor, that's because he has, in fact, served as both in his life's journey. Drink deeply from *Letting Go, Finding You*."

—**Dr. Joshua Graves**, author of *The Simple Secret* and lead minister for Otter Creek Church, Brentwood, TN

"Of the many books on the Enneagram I have read, it would be truthful to say that Hunter Mobley's *Letting Go, Finding You* is my favorite of them all . . . but that feels like underselling it, as it immediately became one of my favorite books on spirituality more broadly. It is tender, wise, and vulnerable, moving effortlessly between Mobley's own story of deep, experiential knowing, and the universal human truths that make authentic change possible for any of us. Theologically informed without being stuffy, and psychologically astute without attempting to be clever, this is a warm, cleansing, clarifying book that will both enable you to name exactly where you are, and give you the resources to go where you want to go. To read this book soulfully and openly is to be transformed."

—**Jonathan Martin**, author of *How to Survive a Shipwreck* and *The Road Away from God*

"*Letting Go, Finding You* deftly weaves the Enneagram with contemplative practices to lighten our spiritual journey as we uncover our beloved selves. Hunter Mobley companions us with warm humor and illuminating wisdom distilled from his touching story. This book is a refreshing and centering breath for our exhausted and overwrought lives. I can't wait to share this with people I love and lead alongside."

—**Christopher Mack**, pastor of Community and Teaching, Vox Veniae, Austin, TX

"Hunter Mobley is a gifted writer, teacher, and pastor. Based on his leadership I have grown immensely in my understanding of the Enneagram as a whole and as it applies to me individually. In this book, not only does Mobley guide us in letting go and finding ourselves; he also helps us become more aware, kind, and thoughtful—which is truly a gift!"

—**Rev. Susan Reed**, associate pastor, Broadway Baptist Church, Louisville, KY

"Who are we when it's not about striving toward becoming something? If you have grown tired of yourself, your striving, your patterned and habitual responses, then this book is for you! Hunter Mobley beckons us home with compassion, wisdom, and deep intention because it's his journey too. In *Letting Go, Finding You*, you too might discover you're not who you think you are, and that's the good news."

—**Alex Reegan**, author of *What Needs to Be Said: Speak Your Truth, Release Shame, Find Oneness*

"Hunter Mobley is an Enneagram master. In this new book, he demonstrates his unique ability to show how the Enneagram is a powerful tool for self-awareness, spiritual growth, healthy relationships, and personal transformation. This is a must-read!"

—**Dr. Clay Stauffer**, senior minister, Woodmont Christian Church, Nashville, TN

"I've read many books on the Enneagram. This one is truly special! Hunter Mobley's words are grounded in experiential wisdom, fearless authenticity, and practiced contemplative Christianity. *Letting Go, Finding You* offers a uniquely illuminated path toward the rediscovery of our innate sacred virtue. With a warm narrative style and a deep commitment to spiritual practice, Mobley has graciously written a practical, stand-out guide for Enneagram exploration and spiritual transformation."

—**A. Dean Stelow**, founder of Reorient Mentoring and host of the Reorient Collective Community

"This book is *the* trifecta: contemplative spirituality, Enneagram wisdom, and a brilliant guide! Hunter Mobley compassionately led me to deepen my understanding of the Love within me, around me, and leading me home. He has now packaged this gift for *you* in these pages. You will be stretched. You will be challenged. And in the end, you will be blessed."

—**Rev. Andy Stoker**, PhD, pastor, Central UMC, Albuquerque

"Hunter Mobley has done something remarkable—he masterfully brings the Enneagram and the contemplative life together in a way that is both profound and accessible. Mobley's clear teaching, humble posture, and courageous authenticity shine throughout these pages. His wisdom reminds us that true spiritual growth isn't about trying harder but about letting go. If you're looking for a guide who integrates contemplative tools with the Enneagram in a beautiful and practical way, this book will be a gift to your soul."

—**Tyler Zach**, author of *The Gospel for Enneagram* devotional series

Letting Go, Finding You

Letting Go, Finding You

Uncover Your Truest Self through the Enneagram and Contemplation

Hunter Mobley

FOREWORD BY SUZANNE STABILE

Broadleaf Books
Minneapolis

LETTING GO, FINDING YOU
Uncover Your Truest Self through the Enneagram and Contemplation

30 29 28 27 26 25 2 3 4 5 6 7 8 9 10

Library of Congress Control Number: 2024945987 (print)

Cover image: © 2024 Getty Images; Small tree grows from dying wood/547539742 by jack-sooksan
Cover design: Broadleaf Books (Brynne Worley)

Print ISBN: 979-8-8898-3165-5
eBook ISBN: 979-8-8898-3166-2

I dedicate this work to my beloved friend and mentor, Rev. Joe Stabile, who has no need to write a book because, like Christ, his life is a living example of the transformation that is possible through the wisdom of the Enneagram and contemplation. Plenty of people around him have taken note, and his lessons have spread throughout the world.

Contents

Foreword by Suzanne Stabile

I first met Hunter Mobley in 2014 while teaching an Enneagram workshop on Gasparilla Island in Florida. My husband, Rev. Joseph Stabile, and I were seated for the celebratory dinner marking the end of the event when Hunter and a friend chose to sit at our table. We found Hunter to be well-read and well-spoken. He was mature beyond his years and relational in a way that offered comfort to all who were seated at our table.

As with most events like this one, I was questioned about the Enneagram, and of course one answer led to another question and another and another. I was intrigued with Hunter's curiosity because he was interested in Enneagram Wisdom beyond just his Personality Type. And though everyone at the table was new to the Enneagram, he had an awareness of other human beings that exceeded his age, and the depth of his questions was beyond the usual.

In the years following our first introduction, I taught on several occasions in Nashville, where Hunter lives. He attended each event, and we managed to find time for coffee or to share a meal. It seemed that the more time we spent together, the more he wanted to learn from me and the more there was to know about him.

During those years, I taught a three-year apprentice program for those who were committed to a long and deep journey through the many facets of Enneagram Wisdom. Hunter applied, and we were pleased to welcome him into the growing community of Life in the Trinity Ministry. As a result, we had an opportunity to get to know him better, and when some years had passed, Joe invited Hunter to join him in teaching a new Cohort, "Enneagram and Contemplative Spirituality," as part of our work at our center in Dallas.

Joe and Hunter are both educated in Enneagram Spiritual Wisdom, and both are theologians and pastors. They have created a learning experience for participants that is now in its eighth year, and some of the fruit from that work has resulted in Hunter writing this beautiful book.

I suppose every person's relationship to the Enneagram is necessarily unique. My journey started when Father Richard Rohr chose to begin teaching me this ancient spiritual wisdom over thirty years ago. While I'm honored to have three books published, I'm a teacher who happens to write books. My husband is a pastor who happens to also teach.

Hunter is a pastor who knows and understands the Enneagram in relation to the theology that is foundational in the Cohort he and Joe lead together. It is where he has developed his expertise in understanding "Passions and Virtues" as taught in ancient Enneagram Spiritual Wisdom, and it is in this book that he has reunited the Enneagram with a spiritual approach.

Honestly, this book is a long time coming. And it could only be written by one who has chosen to be vulnerable enough to allow life to change them in some significant way. In reading parts of Hunter's story throughout the book you will recognize his courage in choices that were, by their very nature, life changing. He writes, "The journey often takes us by surprise and who we become in the process often has more to do with what has happened to us than any undertaking of our own." That is a perfect example of the wisdom in the marriage between the Enneagram and theology.

In the pages that follow, you will be introduced to Enneagram passions and their virtues. And, uncharacteristically for most Enneagram books, you will find that equal attention is paid to both.

Hunter teaches with clarity the journey from virtue to passion and back again, using contemplative living as the cornerstone. He offers for consideration a host of spiritual practices that are both traditional and new. My favorite is simply titled "Stuff."

As you will learn, it turns out that the story, your story, begins in virtue. Quoting Hunter, "Good news comes before the bad. Blessing comes before cursing. The virtues are hidden within us from the very beginning."

It has been my experience that good teachers and accomplished writers of nonfiction have at least this one thing in common. They describe for us things that we know to be true but are unable to name for ourselves. Hunter has been on a long and diligent journey as he worked to understand the intersection between passions, virtues, spiritual practices, and contemplative living.

This lovely book begins with, "The journey is *inward* and not *outward*. We do not need to go outside of ourselves to find what we feel is missing; we need to go deeper inside than we've ever been before to discover that what we've been searching for all along was always there."

And it ends with, "As we let go of old patterns of responding and behaving; as we let go of the false promises that our passions offer to us; as we let go of the false notion that God is far off, disappointed, and waiting for us to find our way back to God; and as we stop trying to save ourselves through steps, penances, and good deeds . . . we will finally find ourselves. We will find our purpose. We will find our virtue. We will uncover and grow our souls."

And I learned from and loved every sentence in between.

—Suzanne Stabile,
author of *The Path Between Us* and
The Journey Toward Wholeness and
host of *The Enneagram Journey* podcast

Introduction

This book has been several years and multiple iterations in the making. After finishing my first book, *40 Days on Being a 2*, published by InterVarsity Press in 2020, I set my sights on writing "my" Enneagram book. A big book seemed like the thing to create for someone like me, someone who loves to write and who travels the country teaching the Enneagram.

As my writing progressed, I had to confront the demon that confronts many nonfiction authors in their first attempt at a full-scale book on the subject that they know the best: how to avoid telling you everything I know about the Enneagram in one book. No one wants to read a textbook, nor is anyone wowed by the depths of Enneagram rabbit holes that my mind can wander into.

As I was putting this book together, I was asked to review or provide endorsements for several other books about the Enneagram by friends and colleagues. Through that work, I discovered that much of the territory of the Enneagram *"and"* has been well traversed. In these finely crafted books, we have seen the wisdom of the Enneagram applied to fundamental disciplines such as work, church, relationships, communication, and discernment.

And so I scrapped my Enneagram writing plans and shifted to the other subject that consumes much of my teaching: contemplative spirituality. I served as a pastor in Nashville for six years and I now coteach an annual year-long program at the Micah Center in Dallas called the Contemplative Cohort; so a book about contemplative spiritualty aligned well with my research and practice.

What I discovered along the way is that when I set out to write an Enneagram book, I ended up writing just as much about contemplative spirituality. And when I decided to just write a spirituality book, I couldn't keep the wisdom of the Enneagram from taking center stage. So, here we are at the blessed intersection of Enneagram wisdom and contemplative spirituality. The two animate each other. This book is about *both-and* and about my journey toward a kinder spirituality—toward my own letting go and finding of myself. What I hope you discover inside this book is my sincere belief that the most meaningful and transformation-inducing Enneagram work can only occur through contemplative spiritual practices. And similarly, some of the best language that we have to describe spiritual transformation uses the lens of the Enneagram—journeying from false self back to true self, from passion back to virtue. We'll dive deeply through this book into the Enneagram passions and virtues, but for now, it is enough to know that the nine Enneagram virtues (of which one is associated with each Enneagram type) are the expressions of the divine inside of us. The passions, in contrast, represent the opposite of each virtue, describing the mask that each Enneagram type wears to keep their precious virtue hidden from the troubles of the world.

The virtue for 1s is serenity, and the passion is anger.
The virtue for 2s is humility, and the passion is pride.
The virtue for 3s is truthfulness, and the passion is deceit.
The virtue for 4s is equanimity, and the passion is envy.
The virtue for 5s is nonattachment, and the passion is greed.
The virtue for 6s is courage, and the passion is fear.
The virtue for 7s is sobriety, and the passion is gluttony.
The virtue for 8s is innocence, and the passion is lust.
The virtue for 9s is action, and the passion is sloth.

The Vincentian order of priests, as the followers of St. Vincent de Paul are known, embody a mantra of living and discernment known as holy delay. Holy delay involves slowing down decision-making long enough for God to surprise with new insight and increased clarity. Practitioners of holy delay make decisions with patience, humility, and intentional slowness. Holy delay is a contemplative spiritual practice (as I will discuss later) by intentionally making room for the Holy to intervene before we launch into our self-determined work and plans.

Holy delay has brought us this book. And while the delay has sometimes felt to me like dying, the delay has been holy nonetheless. Holy delay has given me the clarity to author a book about the beautiful interconnectedness of Enneagram wisdom and contemplative spiritual practices. Through my own unwitting journey of holy delay, I have become convinced that the best way to understand our journey of spiritual evolution from false self to true self is through the words and wisdom of the Enneagram and that the only way to do the Enneagram work of moving from false self to true self successfully is through a lifelong commitment to living as a contemplative. Thank God for holy delay.

In Benedictine spirituality, practitioners, even ones who have been studying and following St. Benedict's tenets for years, have a simple mantra: *always a beginner*. The nuanced invitation to incorporating beginner status into the framing of our spiritual lives is recognizing that simple truths that can be understood by children, returned to over time, are more often the agents of lasting change than esoteric mysteries that can be understood by only a few.

We are all beginners. And every day we begin again.

What Is the Enneagram?

The Enneagram is a personality system describing nine different ways of seeing and responding to the world. The Enneagram stands alongside many helpful personality tools and inventories, like Myers-Briggs, StrengthsFinder, DISC, and Birkman. In my first year of college, I encountered a personality-typing system that helped us discover whether our personalities could be best described as a lion, otter, tiger, or golden retriever. *Any other golden retrievers out there?!*

The name Enneagram simply puts two Greek words together: *ennea*, meaning "nine," and *gram*, meaning

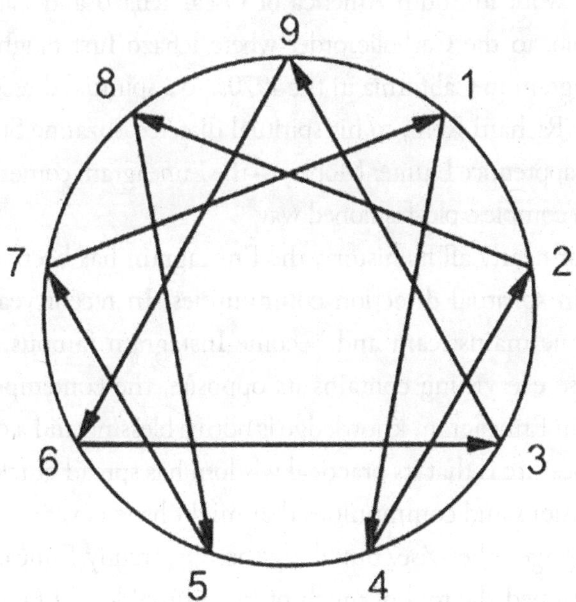

Figure 1. The Enneagram.[1]

“figure.” So, the Enneagram is a figure with nine numbers around it, representing nine distinct personality styles.

The Enneagram comes to us cloaked in mystery. We don’t have a clear origin point or a linear arc of how the personality theory developed. Instead, the Enneagram is a tool that has developed and spread from teacher to student through many centuries. We believe the tool began through the work of Evagrius Ponticus, specifically through the language of his nine passions, and students of his who came later. The Enneagram was not developed in a methodical, organized way. Enneagram wisdom has no universal authority. From Ponticus to Pope Gregory I to Sufi Muslims to desert mothers and fathers trying to live out a reimagined Christianity outside of the Roman Empire, to the work in South America of Oscar Ichazo and Claudio Naranjo, to the Catholic order where Ichazo first taught the Enneagram in California in the 1970s, to a spiritual director of Father Richard Rohr, to his spiritual directee Suzanne Stabile, to her apprentice Hunter Mobley—the Enneagram comes to us in this complex, old-fashioned way.

For nearly all its history, the Enneagram has been a tool used in spiritual direction communities. In recent years, it has gone mainstream and become Instagram famous. And because everything contains its opposite, the contemporary surge in Enneagram knowledge is both a blessing and a curse. The blessing is that its practical wisdom has spread quickly to generations and communities that might have never accessed its message otherwise. But along the way, trendy Enneagram has stripped the tool of much of its spiritual lens. I take and enjoy the opportunities to share the Enneagram in corporate and nonspiritual settings, but my messaging always feels truncated, and I fear that without a spiritual application, its impact on students may be short-lived. That's why, in this book, I've reunited the Enneagram with a spiritual approach.

The Enneagram does not belong to one spiritual system or religion. The Enneagram supports any spiritual tradition promoting a message that something of eternity is inside each one of us. Whether you believe in something akin to an essence, a soul, a true self, or a Christ inside, my language will feel accessible and familiar. I write from a spirituality that sets a place for all of us to sit around one table, together with our disagreements, questions, and doubts.

One of the simplest and most profound gifts that the Enneagram gives to us is a set of words to describe us to ourselves and to others.

Several years ago, there was a reemergence of interest in Mister Rogers. In the United States, we were about to enter one of our most contentious election cycles in modern history, and somehow the cultural zeitgeist knew we needed to reacquaint ourselves with an old neighborhood friend. Two films were released during the period I am describing: one a documentary called *Won't You Be My Neighbor?* (2018) and the other a biopic called *A Beautiful Day in the Neighborhood* (2019) starring Tom Hanks as Fred Rogers. I loved them both. As a child who grew up watching *Mister Rogers' Neighborhood*, I was so happy to see a reintroduction to an old friend.

The biopic includes a scene where Mister Rogers is holding vigil at the bedside of a dying man, along with several of the man's family members. Like many of us walking through that liminal moment of life, the family members in the film are saying the things we say when we don't know what else to say. They tell their father that they can't wait until he is well enough to take that trip he has always wanted to take. They tell him they're so excited to build new memories together when he gets up. They simply aren't ready to attend to the gravity and the weight of what is really happening: the imminent death of their beloved father. Fred Rogers, in his wisdom, stands to the side, observing, and during a break in the conversation he says: "*What can be mentioned can be managed.*" Fred is trying to help the family realize that by telling the truth about what is really occurring, everything becomes more manageable and welcome for both them and for their father.

The Enneagram gives us language to tell the truth about ourselves with the goal of managing our personalities better so that they stop managing us. The language of the passions and the virtues, which will be the primary lens through which this book explores the Enneagram, gives us the first seeds to managing ourselves in such a way that we can rediscover how to live from our virtue instead of our passion. All Enneagram teaching, wisdom, and literature is offered in service of mentioning things about ourselves with a goal of better self and soul management.

What Is Contemplative Spirituality?

Later in the book, I will explore contemplative spirituality in depth and the practices that are involved, but here at the beginning, I want to demystify the concept for those readers, like me, whose spiritual backgrounds did not use words like *contemplative*. Note that throughout the book, I will use the terms *contemplation*, *contemplative living*, and *contemplative spirituality* interchangeably.

I grew up in the Southern Baptist Church in Nashville, Tennessee. The spiritual practices that I encountered and practiced in my early spiritual formation were typical of my background: worship, Bible study, active prayer (you know—with church-secretary–prepared lists and such), evangelism, and good old-fashioned spiritual hustle. I'm grateful for the years of Bible drills, mission trips, and Sunday school, which all offered me a foundation for my spiritual life today, even if my original system of belief is no longer large enough to contain my current spiritual journey. We are all products of our raisings and are limited in spiritual understanding and expression by what the community around us practices. I did not learn rhythms like fasting, ordering spirituality around a liturgical calendar, meditation, and silence. The practices that we valued in my corner of the Baptist world were more active, designed to increase our knowledge and experience of God (worship, Bible study, Sunday schools) and perform good works in our community on behalf of God (evangelism, mission, outreach).

A spirituality that is contemplative in practice does not undo or undervalue these active practices. Contemplative spirituality is a different way of experiencing God, one that is less active and more open, making room for God's unseen and sometimes mysterious work in our lives and in our world. Contemplative spirituality is less about what we can do for God and more about making space for God to rearrange our hearts, minds, and bodies in ways that connect us to eternal things. Contemplative spiritual practices open us up to the inherent holiness of the present moment and free us from making our own way to God by recognizing that God is always present and working whether we notice or not.

In the church of my childhood, we didn't use the language of contemplative spirituality, but there were small clues that some of us were learning its message. The late Dottie Rambo, who was a member of the church in Nashville that I pastored, penned a Southern gospel song called "The Unseen Hand." We sang its lyrics: "I'm trusting to the Unseen Hand that guides me through this weary land," bearing witness to a fundamental contemplative notion that God is always about God's business and our business is simply to attend.[2]

Contemplative spirituality does not belong to one religion. You can be a contemplative Christian, a contemplative Jew, or a contemplative Muslim. Contemplative practices are also central to non-Western faiths, like Buddhism and Hinduism. A life of contemplation is an approach to spirituality that contrasts with expressions of spirituality that are about *our* work, *our* study, *our* knowing, and *our* success. Contemplative spirituality offers an approach that is frankly less taxing and less results oriented. Rarely do contemplatives expect observable or measurable spiritual outcomes.

Contemplative practices bear fruit that grows gradually until one day we are surprised by the transformation that we notice in our lives.

The Christian story animates and informs my spiritual journey. You may have found another way of making meaning from the spiritual life, and that's wonderful. My goal is not to convince you of the Christian story but to convince you that a lived spiritual practice that is honest and true to your story is necessary to guide you from your passion back to your virtue. I will use some of the language of my Christian story because that is the language I have to offer, but you should apply the spiritual story that fits your journey and is exactly right for you.

My hope and prayer are that you will find the crumbs from my journey and my introduction to contemplative spirituality and Enneagram wisdom helpful in your own journey to letting go and finding you in the great, universal center of God—providing a gateway to a transformed life.

1

Why Five-Step Spirituality Is No Longer Working

My childhood church offered Bible drills beginning in the fourth grade, and I couldn't wait to be a part of them. *Attention, draw swords!* was the way that each competition began as the judge called us to stand tall and present our Bibles in front of our chests—right hand over the back of the Bible and left hand over the front. At our first Sunday night gathering, all the fourth graders were given the choice of whether we wanted to memorize verses from the King James Version (KJV) of the Bible or the New International Version (NIV; a more updated modern language translation), and for some reason that I cannot now justify, I chose the KJV. *You know*, the one with all the thees and thous and witherests. I was the only fourth grader who chose the KJV translation! I was not even at one of the King James–only Baptist churches, but for some reason I was a King James–only ten-year-old.

If you are on the evangelical deconstructing and reconstructing journey, like me, you might understand my mixed feelings as I look back on my teenage and early adult commitment to spread the gospel through what look to me now like means of mixed motives. In college, I joined an evangelical campus ministry, Campus Outreach. I even became president of the organization during my senior year. My time in college ministry was a fun and bonding experience, but like so many campus ministry types, we took our religion seriously. In the mornings, we had "quiet times" that consisted of studying the Scripture in step-by-step ways. As we learned the method, ministry leaders encouraged us to turn in our quiet times to more senior students, who would give us feedback on whether we were making accurate observations, interpretations, and applications.

The hallmark of our campus ministry was the summer beach project. We rented an entire motel in the heart of Myrtle Beach, South Carolina. Sixty of us lived at the Holiday South Motel for three months while we worked at various fast-food restaurants across the area, becoming part of the seasonal help that is necessary to sustain a beachfront town in the summer. During my summer beach project, I worked at Bojangles as the backline cook, making dirty rice, green beans, and macaroni and cheese. The work was sweaty and fast-paced, and I loved it. In the evenings and on Saturdays, we got down to the real point of the summer mission: beach evangelism. We dispersed in pairs to walk the beach and initiate conversations with individuals and families about our understanding of the Christian story—all in hopes of swaying them to adopt our doctrine. As an Enneagram 2 who is more practiced at winning people to myself rather than to a cause, I was not a good beach evangelist. I struck up some friendly conversations with sunbathers who had the patience to meet a stranger, focusing more on casual banter than proselytizing. I hoped the beach project leaders were not observing my underzealousness.

I was more comfortable building relationships with my coworkers at Bojangles. I made some good friends that summer and was able to get Fronnie and Miss Rhonda—two of my new friends—to join our end-of-summer dinner and worship night. Was I immersing myself in a new experience that summer, working in a restaurant kitchen, opening myself to the things that I might learn from my new friendships? Or did I see myself as part of God's great army, sent to teach people less fortunate than me how to lift themselves through the story of Christian exceptionalism and empire? My sense, unfortunately, is the latter.

After college and law school, I continued to follow the script of working hard for Jesus, believing that I was not only capable but also destined to do important things for God. I taught Sunday school, served on my church's board of directors, sang in the choir, went on mission trips, read daily devotionals, and hosted evangelistic dinners at my home. Eventually, I became the executive pastor at my church—a final development that was the inevitable conclusion of all my striving for God. Along the way, I made great friends, fell in love with the messy hope of the local church, and tried earnestly to become a person of integrity and wisdom. If the spiritual axiom that "everything contains its opposite" is true, then I must be honest enough to see the good that a devoted evangelical experience brought me. But I can also see how the fear of disappointing God and diverging from the group norm kept me busy in a spiritual life that seemed hard. There were lots of rules to follow and the path was slippery.

One Sunday morning, sitting in the choir loft, I reflected on the upcoming season of Lent and realized that I needed to decide what I was going to give up for the forty days between Ash Wednesday and Easter. My earliest church homes did not memorialize the liturgical calendar except for an acknowledgment of Advent. We hung the garland around the church sanctuary in early December and placed an Advent wreath on the "In Remembrance of Me" table, but we did not make special occasions of Lent, Pentecost, All Saints' Day, or Ordinary Time. But the church of my early adulthood—the one that I would eventually pastor—had begun to emphasize the seasons of the church calendar and I was preparing to attend my first Ash Wednesday service.

Sitting in the choir loft that Sunday morning, I thought through the usual suspects for Lenten fasts. Caffeine? Chocolate? As I was running through the litany of typical fasting options, two words formed in my mind: *cease striving*. I would like to think that these words came from the deepest parts of me, the parts that represent the interwoven, tangled-up truest self and the part of God that lives inside me. *Cease striving.* The words were not familiar. They did not represent a mantra or a determined declaration that I had been contemplating. *Cease striving.* The words represented the cry of my soul. My soul, which had in many ways been buried beneath obligations and expectations, was crying out for some more room. *For some rest.* My soul could not take one more denial of myself, disguised as obligation to God. For my first Lenten journey, I needed to do less, not more.

For my Lenten fast, I needed to learn some things of God that can be learned only in silence, stillness, solitude, and subtraction. Sometimes even our fasting can feel like an addition—addition of a new habit or a new thing to work hard at and get frustrated with ourselves about.

Fasting is a classical spiritual discipline, and at its core, fasting represents the most contemplative of emphases: when we cut out something nonessential, we make more room for the essential things to emerge. But for me, as a twenty-five-year-old who wanted desperately to be good (*maybe because I didn't think that I was really all that good—but more to come on that later*), fasting was just another way of bearing out a spirituality that was focused on getting God's attention and approval. I had made myself the hero of the story. Because I was doing important things for God, I deserved God's attention, and once I had God's attention, I believed that God would do something genuinely great with my life. One of the greatest sins that I must work on still is putting to death the burden of Christian exceptionalism. My Christian experience had told me that I was destined to be great. That God wanted me to be great. That God was going to make me great.

How much pain and trouble has been wrought in our world—and in my world—by those of us who believe we are soldiers for God. In *Leaving Church*, Barbara Brown Taylor writes: "As a general rule, I would say that human beings never behave more badly toward one another than when they believe they are protecting God."[1] I would add to Taylor's assertion that human beings never behave more badly toward *themselves* than when they believe they are protecting God. Not only had I inevitably hurt others in my quest for an elusive holiness standard I had adopted by inheritance, but I was also constantly at war with myself.

Cease striving. I still hear those words rising from the deepest stirring of my soul, as clearly as I heard them on my first Lenten journey fifteen years ago. My Lenten commitment that year was a wonderful, life-giving one. I committed to do less, not more. Worry less, not more. The commitment went beyond just my spiritual life. As an Enneagram 2, I spend a lot of time worrying about friendships. Have I invested enough? Do my friends really know that I am there for them? Am I still indispensable to my friends, or have I done something to allow the relationship to become less sticky, putting me at risk for the discard pile? These questions cause me to exhaust myself with a Monday-to-Sunday barrage of coffees, lunches, and dinners. And when I do allow some time for myself, I mostly spend the time worrying about connections that I have neglected and how I can reach out to reengage the other person.

There was—and unfortunately, is—so much striving in my life. I need my *cease striving* mantra every day, not just the forty blessed days before Easter.

Many factors have motivated my lifetime of striving. Certainly, my background in the evangelical South, and the Baptist church specifically, carried all the said and unsaid expectations of an active spirituality of good works and personal holiness. But there were other factors at play for me too. Personal motivations. Parts of myself that I was so scared to let see the light of day, and so they had to remain hidden and covered beneath a steady stream of church activities and spiritual work. Your story may not be the same as mine, but I am guessing that if you came up in a conservative expression of religion, parts of your innermost being might also make you afraid. Afraid that if some of your innermost desires or thoughts were known, they would misalign with the values of your community of origin, and so, like me, you kept them at bay.

In our early lives, we are family and community fragments, naturally adopting many of the beliefs and strategies of our familial and spiritual ancestors. But adulthood and spiritual evolution invite us to become less of a family fragment and more of a whole individual, capable of finding our own true north.

From the time that I was six or seven years old, I knew that I was different from the other boys my age. I was the opposite of a natural athlete. I excelled in music and theater experiences—my father and I were in a summer theater troupe where, as a four-year-old, I played the changeling child in *A Midsummer Night's Dream* on the front lawn of Cheekwood Estate in Nashville. My cousin Grace was my best friend and we loved playing dress-up from the hamper of her mother's old clothes. But I quickly noticed the cues that my behavior bumped up against the norm.

My mother brought me some of my grandfather's old suits to add to our dress-up collection, much to my disappointment. My cousin's grandfather refused to buy six-year-old me stick-on pink fingernails on a *pick-out-whatever-you-want* trip to the Dollar Store. And when someone asked first-grader me whom I would like to marry, I naively said that I guessed I would get married to my best friend, Tom.

People in the late 1980s and early 1990s in Nashville were not ready for a gay kid and so I learned to tone down any awareness of my sexuality as much as I could, though not all that well, I suspect. I adopted the strategy of being helpful and kind as a way of earning love from people whom I was not sure would be able to love the real me. So much of my helpfulness, kindness, courteousness, and successful performance has been a strategy to bank goodwill with loved ones so that if they ever discovered that I was gay, the goodwill would outweigh the withdrawal of having a gay son, a gay family member, or a gay friend.

I doubled down on Christian practice and church participation because religion gave me a place to belong and something that I could be good at. I also found comfort in the Christian themes of redemptive suffering, denial of self, and thorns in one's side. "For whosoever will save his life shall lose it: and whosoever will lose his life for my sake shall find it" (Matthew 16:25 KJV).

In my early twenties, I tried the now-debunked strategy of conversion therapy, with the highest hopes that I could finally just be normal. But the therapy did not change the way I felt or remove the deep longings inside me. Soon after, I learned the semantic nuance of describing what I experienced as same-sex attraction rather than something as serious as gayness, and I found some community with other men who had adopted that language. I didn't feel as alone, and I was able to talk to people—even to my pastor—about the thorn in my side that I could now name publicly but only because any naming of my desires was quickly followed by the community's expected commitment to celibacy or trying to marry a wife. I suspect we were all half-hearted. In retrospect, I am grateful that most of the people in my Christian community with whom I shared my secret seemed to be following *my* lead in underacknowledging my gayness rather than coaching me toward any underacknowledgment of it. I am fortunate that cultural and denominational changes occurred during my twenties that made more room for conversation and understanding around human sexuality.

I began dipping my toes in communities that held more progressive convictions about sexuality, even though it would be years still before I could embrace my own. As a law student at New York University, I became a part of

First Presbyterian Church on Fifth Avenue in Greenwich Village. First Church was the closest church to my dormitory, and I found some comfort in the Presbyterian theology and practice that I had first learned in college at Davidson, a Presbyterian enclave. First Church had two openly gay ministers on its staff, which was both comforting and conflicting for me.

After I moved back to Nashville and joined the staff of Christ Church as its executive pastor, many of my colleagues and I found ourselves on a spiritual journey of evolution as we discovered the work of Phyllis Tickle, Henri Nouwen, Tony Campolo, Richard Rohr, Barbara Brown Taylor, and Brian McLaren. Gradually, our beliefs moved toward greater inclusion. And as my thinking and believing evolved, I had a harder and harder time justifying a life closed to the desires and intimacies that I had sensed were an inextricable part of myself since as early as I could remember. And so, toward the end of my six years as pastor at Christ Church, I knew that the time had come to finally leave the boundaries of evangelicalism and inhabit an integrated life where my living and my evolved believing could finally unite. A place where I could finally discover and be myself, for the first time. *Letting go and finding me.*

I had to cease striving to be somebody that I was never going to be. I had to cease striving to be anything less than who I knew myself to be in the deepest places of my knowingness.

All the books and step-by-step methods of overcoming gayness never worked for me. Working harder and trying more at my spirituality gained me friends inside my closed community, but these connections came at a deep cost to my soul as I increasingly separated from my truest self.

I am describing my journey, and though yours is different and may have nothing to do with sexuality, I'm betting that you have found, like me, that whatever you have tried to will and work away through a rigid spirituality that demanded active attention to steps and methods and predictive outcomes didn't work all that well. *Five-step spirituality does not work.* The spiritual disciplines that have made the most difference in my life did not involve trying harder but instead surrendering and letting go.

Several years ago, I was traveling to a church to lead a weekend Enneagram teaching event and I found myself in the Southwest ticket line as B52. Obviously, I had neglected to either pay the extra fee for an A-list pass or curate my prior day to check-in online exactly twenty-four hours before my flight, so I joined the anxious B- and C-listers, who were all wondering whether there would be any room in the overhead bins. Standing in line in front of me—*B51, I presumed*—was a man reading a book. The rest of us were actively readying ourselves to board and trying hard not to let anyone dart in front of us in line, but the man in front of me seemed immune to our anxious preoccupation. He remained fixated on his reading. As our time to scan boarding passes finally arrived, he placed a marker between the pages and closed his book, and I was able to get my first glimpse of the title that had transfixed my fellow traveler:

Right Away and All at Once: Five Steps to Transform Your Business and Enrich Your Life.

What a title! And it represents so much of what we expect in life and in spirituality. We want to have everything right away and we want to have it all at once. And we want there to be steps. *And we want there to only be five of them!* Since my experience in the Southwest ticket line that day, I have used this anecdote to introduce my Know Your Number teaching for Enneagram 3s, who are hard-charging to meet their goals in the most efficient ways possible. But the cultural zeitgeist tempts all of us with spiritual scripts that promise guaranteed outcomes right away and all at once.

The spiritual life is not a right-away-and-all-at-once experience. And much to our mutual frustration, we will not find any surefire steps. The spiritual life involves more of God's doing to us and less of our doing toward God. If there had been steps to follow to overcome my gayness (which I now see as something to celebrate rather than overcome), for most of my life I would have given everything that I had to discover them. There were so many prayer services, therapy appointments, books, and altar calls where I earnestly prayed for a change to happen in my sexuality right away and all at once. But the change never came. Instead, change occurred in me when I exchanged my five-step spiritual programs for a process of surrendering and letting go. And when I finally surrendered to a process of less rather than more, I discovered that the transformation that I really needed and wanted was an alignment of my life with my true self and a letting go of all the masks and projections that I had adopted in unsuccessful attempts to cut out a part of my intrinsic humanity.

Grinning and bearing it, with clenched fists and bulging knuckles, is not getting us anywhere. We need to exchange our five-step programs and quick fixes for something different. Something rooted in ancient tradition and the patience of time. Something that can truly bring the change and transformation that we are really looking for. To be clear, I'm not opposed to the idea of "steps" altogether. For example, many people have found freedom in Bill W.'s twelve-step program for recovery from addiction, but even though the program contains steps, they do not happen immediately or easily. Very few of the steps involve outer work; most of the steps are about moving deeper into an interior journey of union with God and integrated living.

Results-driven approaches to spirituality are like a drug. We find ourselves needing more and more to get the same high. Our search for a series of steps to take to unlock our spiritual potential is another way for us to remain in control of our spiritual lives. Another way to build our egos. Another way to replace God with self. When we cling to control, we remain stuck in the illusion that we oversee our spiritual growth and development. Our programs are leading us from disappointment to disappointment as we find ourselves constantly needing the next book, the next guru, the next system, and the next set of steps. All true spirituality is about letting go. Less, not more. Subtracting, not adding. If we are ever going to find a way off the treadmill of consumer spirituality, we need to discover a path that helps us release control.

When I was pastoring at Christ Church, we oriented our preaching around the lectionary calendar as part of our journey to discover and try on spiritual rhythms and practices that were bigger than our time, context, and culture. In lectionary preaching, sermons are based on specific predetermined texts that Christian churches across denominations and geographies are following on the same Sunday. Preaching by the lectionary calendar is also a helpful way for preachers to avoid returning repeatedly to the same candy-stick passages that we love, while also avoiding difficult Scriptures. Following the lectionary ensures that we all get our yearly dose of some violent, bloody psalms, requiring us to wrestle with how to place passages about divorce and fornication into a modern context that includes insights and revelations into the times and cultures of Scripture authors.

One week, as I began sermon preparation for an upcoming Sunday, I turned to the lectionary passages for the day. I was thrilled to find that the New Testament passage was from Romans 5, one of the great poems of Scripture. In the Pauline letter to the church in Rome, the poetic prose reads: "Suffering produces endurance, and endurance produces character, and character produces hope (Romans 5:3–4 ESV)." I scribbled a sermon title, "The Road to Hope," at the top of my legal pad, eager to spend the next few days discerning the necessary steps to take on each phase of the journey from suffering to hope. My plan was to map out the steps to take from suffering to endurance then turn to the steps to take from endurance to character, and finally to discover the steps from character to hope. I was sure to have a triumph on my hands. If I could distill and describe a step-by-step roadmap from suffering to hope, then I would be well on my way to becoming the guru that I so wanted my congregation to applaud.

The problem came almost immediately the next day as I devoted some hours to really dig into the passage and supporting commentaries. The word that described the link between each stop along the journey from suffering to hope was *produces.* Other translations use the phrases "brings forth" or "develops" or "worketh" to describe the link between suffering and endurance, endurance and character, and character and hope. These words and phrases suggest a process that naturally occurs. One thing leads to the other, as if the journey is destined to happen.

I was struggling to discern where my place was and what steps I could take in each leg of the journey. If suffering produces endurance, then what steps are necessary? If endurance produces character, then is there anything for us to do? And if character produces hope, do we have to *make* anything happen?

I panicked. It was already Thursday and my sermon was not coming together. I could not mine any steps along the journey that turned out to be a passive process, a process that was more of an undergoing than an undertaking. My plan to discern and describe each clearly defined step in the process from suffering to hope seemed doomed.

Finally, the light bulb flashed on, and I learned from the passage one single step, not a series of results-oriented processes to get us to hope (*right away and all at once!*). To me, the passage invited one single, solitary step in our journey from suffering to hope: *don't avoid the suffering.*

If we attend to the suffering and don't employ our usual strategies of avoidance and deflection, whether that's mentally escaping, eating, spending, shopping, drinking, or numbing, the suffering will have its journey in us. And the suffering will produce in us endurance and eventually character and finally hope—one of the eternal things, along with faith and love, that never passes away. The problem for me and I am guessing for you is that we don't like suffering very much. Right now, in American culture, the church is divided between congregations that see their path forward as joining Jesus in his suffering and those that are fixated on being God's armor bearers by bringing a sword to culture in reaction to the culture's waning interest in Christian religion.

I have all kinds of ways to avoid suffering. On my last Sunday as a pastor at Christ Church, in 2019, feelings of loss and anxiety clouded my mind. Even though the transition was planned, and the congregation was kindly preparing a cupcake social in the fellowship hall to see me off, I was struggling with core questions of identity: Who will I be when I am no longer Christ Church's pastor? To whom will I belong? To whom will I matter? How will I carry out a sense of calling and purpose in a new phase of life without an official office of ministry?

As the service moved forward, I became increasingly uncomfortable by my growing awareness that Monday would bring gut-wrenching questions of identity. And so, instead of sitting with my suffering—*because who chooses that, right?!*—I decided to give myself a fix of something that was sure to numb me to the pain of my approaching existential crisis. I turned to the most well-practiced avoidance technique in my personal quiver: I found somebody to save. Somebody to rescue. Somebody to need me.

There was a man in our church whom I will name here as James. He had been coming to my Sunday school class for a year and had been becoming more integrated into the life of our community. But he dealt with a mental health journey that led him to some dire financial challenges that resulted in him living in the Nashville Rescue Mission for men. A group of very faithful members of our church, including a staff person who worked under my direction to help steward pastoral care and benevolence ministry, had been working with James for several months to help him find housing, work, and some long-term sustainable solutions to the problems that had resulted in his current homelessness.

But that morning in Sunday school, James had come, as he faithfully did week after week, with a nasty head cold. He told the group that some serious flu was raging through the mission and that he feared that his cold was developing into it. These were months before any of us had heard the words *coronavirus* or *COVID-19*, but still, his cold seemed serious to me.

While people were lining up to take Communion, I snaked my way through the pews to where James was sitting. Once I was in earshot, I leaned down and told him that if he wanted, after the service, I would drive him to an extended stay hotel so he could get out of the mission for the next week. I told him that I did not want him in the mission while his head cold was intensifying and flu was raging through. He thanked me and, after the service and cupcake send-off, I drove him to a local extended-stay inn and checked him in for the week.

The problem is that my motives were not pure. I was trying to help myself more than I was trying to help James. Getting involved with his situation was the fix I needed to remind myself that I was necessary in people's lives and that even after my job as pastor had ended, I could still be the indispensable person for others. The deeper problem was that my intervention in his life was at odds with the thoughtful longer-term help that several members of my congregation, including a member of my staff, were making for James. His week in the extended stay hotel created confusing and painful outcomes when the week ended and the other solutions were still in the works, meaning that I would either pay for another week or see him return to the mission. He ended up staying at the inn for a few weeks, but life eventually brought him back to the mission before some of the plans that he and the members of our church were mutually working toward came to fruition.

Helping, fixing, and rescuing are my go-to strategies for avoiding suffering. Yours are probably different and, like me, may result from some of your core woundings and the motivations of your Enneagram type. But many of us are unaccustomed to welcoming the suffering and doing the deeper spiritual work to incorporate the suffering into our stories and into our maturing. But, as Romans 5 reminds us, it is only through attendance to our suffering that we will find our way toward endurance, character, and hope.

And so, in a world—and particularly, a spirituality—that offers us five-step solutions to change our lives, alleviate our suffering, and maximize our potential, *right away and all at once*, the wisdom journey invites us to a different framework. A path that is kinder, gentler, simpler, *and so much harder*: staying present to our suffering long enough for the suffering to bear the fruit of endurance and character and hope in our lives.

I hope that, like me, you are ready to embrace a spiritual path integrated to your truest self so you can be present to pain and suffering. If we accept suffering's invitations, we will find our way toward an integrated, honest, and authentic spirituality that is kinder to ourselves and honors others at the same time. If we are going to be people who are becoming wise while our spirituality matures, we must abandon our pursuit of quick fixes. We must give up our search for the next book, the next conference, or the next guru who can distill our problems and our spiritual quests into step-by-step processes accomplished in our timing and by our own grit.

The spiritualities that hold up across an entire lifetime of an individual—providing meaning-making in not one season of life but in many—are those that allow suffering, those that let go of control, and those that surrender to the unseen work of God in our lives. Let's free ourselves from the functional atheism, as Father Richard Rohr describes in *The Naked Now*, that tells us if anything good is going to happen in our lives that it is going to be a result of our actions. Let's instead submit ourselves to the unraveling and undergoing work of God. A work that is God's and not ours. A work that invites us simply to attend and intend.

2

The Goal Is Transformation, Not Change

Wisdom traditions, including many stories contained in the Christian Bible, often characterize the spiritual life through the metaphor of journey. Spiritual practices like pilgrimage invite us to discover insights about ourselves along the way that we could never have learned at home. The steps that we take in pursuit of spiritual fruit are not always predictable and the paths are rarely straight. The journey often takes us by surprise, and who we become in the process often has more to do with what has happened to us than any undertaking of our own.

One of the reasons this book exists is because of a pilgrimage I took over ten years ago. My college roommate,

Chad, was getting married in Oxford, England, to someone whom he had met while they were both graduate students abroad. Several of us traveled from America to Oxford for the ceremony. Chad and Grace's wedding was just the excuse that I needed to visit the small town outside of London where I had spent a semester abroad in high school. The time that I spent there as a seventeen-year-old boarding student thousands of miles away from my home in Nashville was formative in every way possible. Ten years later, I was eager to step back into my past for a brief visit and perhaps rediscover some of my seventeen-year-old self.

On that trip, while I was resting in a coffee shop outside of Harrod's in London, I struck up a casual conversation with a local woman who was interested in my American accent. During our conversation, she said, "You're a writer, aren't you?"

I told her that I was not, and she responded, "Oh, that's funny, I would have sworn that you were a writer. Oh well."

We went on to speak for a few more minutes before I left the coffee shop. For some reason, that woman's question stayed with me for the next couple of days. I did love writing, but I had stopped for some reason. The busyness of life and building a career had led me away from my love for writing. I began making notes in a journal during that trip: those notes became essays, and those essays became some of the writing that has led to this book.

I had to take a pilgrimage to England—on what I thought was only a nostalgic trip down memory lane—to remember that I loved to write and to reawaken the inner knowledge that writing is something I can't not do. The most important insight from my British pilgrimage is that the seed to write was buried deep inside of me. The desire to write was already there—not something new but something old—connected to the truest parts of my innermost self. As T. S. Eliot describes: "And at the end of all our exploring will be to arrive where we started and to know the place for the first time."[1]

In *The Great Spiritual Migration*, Brian McLaren says that the most important story of the Hebrew Bible is the story of God telling Abram, before God changed his name to Abraham, to get up, get moving, and head to a new land that has yet to be revealed to him.[2] According to McLaren, God repeatedly invited biblical characters to embark on an uncomfortable journey, both literally and metaphorically, to expand their understanding and experience true transformation. Abram parted with his family and headed off for places unknown. Joseph was beaten by his brothers, shoved in a pit, sold to Midianites, thrown in jail, and eventually wound up as a high-ranking public official. Ruth left her family of origin, joined her mother-in-law's family, and was surprised to find love, security, and home. Jesus left home and set out for the desert toward a pruning experience to ready him for public ministry. The disciples all left parents and siblings to follow a new and captivating leader on uncertain journeys.

The journeys of these biblical characters and my own journey to England all awakened something in the pilgrim. The contemplative journey is God's rearranging of our circumstances in such a way that we can meet ourselves—our true selves—new, as if for the first time.

In classical Enneagram teaching, expert teachers use the distinguishing language of true self and false self. The concept of false self is equated with personality, or Enneagram type. The idea is that there is something less than whole, something masking, something untrue about the personalities that we project. Personality theory is embedded with the idea that the personalities that we project are less than fully reflective of whatever is truest about us. Our Enneagram type summarizes our personality, and our personality is the adaptation that we wear to cover what's truest and most vulnerable from the unkind analyses of the world around us.

True self is the language of the soul or essence of a person. When I first began learning Enneagram wisdom, I ignored the language of the true-self–false-self distinction because of the connotations I brought to the word *false*. As Enneagram teachers, we are quick to remind people that our personalities are not bad, and they do not carry any moral weight. No Enneagram numbers are especially good, and no Enneagram numbers are especially bad. And even though our personalities can hurt us or get us into trouble, they can help us as well. For example, while it is true that my desire for appreciation causes me to intervene in lives that have not solicited my help, it's just as true that my ability to discover and predict other people's feelings allows me to respond with an empathy that many cannot muster. If the Enneagram teaches us anything, it is that two things can be true and that everything contains its opposite.

Still, I recoiled at the idea of a false self. Maybe it was just the shame of my performative three-wing, but admitting that my personality—described through my Enneagram type—is my false self felt like a betrayal of all the goodness that my personality brings to me and to my relationships. My personality is an integrated part of my self and to try to escape my personality would be to cut off a part of who I know myself to be.

But the language of the false self does not carry any moral weight. Our personalities are false selves not because they are wrong or bad but because they are the masks we wear covering our true selves. Later, we'll examine the language of the Enneagram passions and virtues to discover the ways in which our false selves are just the opposites of our true selves, but for right now, it's enough to understand that we use the language of false self to describe our Enneagram numbers as a way of learning that we contain something deeper and truer than our personalities. We have a true self buried beneath the layers of our false self. Behind and beyond our personalities are souls—true selves, essences. Our spiritual journeys invite us to dig through the layers of false self and uncover what lies beneath.

But here's the important point: we do not build or create our true selves; we simply rediscover our true selves. The journey is *inward* and not *outward*. We do not need to go outside of ourselves to find what we feel is missing; we need to go deeper inside than we've ever been before to discover that what we've been searching for all along was always there.

Across time and culture, we tell the same stories. Many of our ancient fables and myths feature someone embarking on a journey to find happiness, courage, or meaning, only to discover along the way that these things were already deep inside of them. Validation comes from the remembering and revealing of what was always true, which is that deep inside of us is something eternal, connected to all things that have lived, are living, and ever will live. But our souls remained untended in the world of false self and ego-building.

Before we move further in our journey from false self back to true self, it is important to distinguish between two essential (but easy to conflate) concepts: change and transformation.

I have heard my mentors Joe and Suzanne Stabile, who are spiritual wisdom teachers based in Dallas, Texas, teach about the difference between change and transformation so many times that the distinction has become fundamental to my spiritual journey. Change occurs when we take on something new or decide to make a shift in our life that involves hard work. If we decide to improve our fitness, change our behavior, or put a new discipline into practice, we often must work hard, take on new habits and activities, and fight through some mental and physical hurdles to reach our goal. Change is tough. But many times, change is necessary. And the spiritual life involves opportunities and seasons of change.

Transformation, however, is a different thing. Transformation is a process of letting old things fall away. In the work of transformation, as old things fall away, what remains has the opportunity to reemerge. Spirituality is more a work of transformation than a work of change. Change suggests that we oversee our outcomes and realities. Transformation, on the other hand, suggests that some process outside of our striving is at work and that if we open our hands rather than clench our fists, what is left can shine through.

Many of our efforts to change our lives build our false selves, while the work of transformation dismantles them. The Enneagram invites us into a transformative journey from passion (or false self) to virtue (or true self). And the pathway for the journey is a contemplative spiritual practice that allows old things—namely, our passion—to fall away so that what has always been there can reemerge and shine through: our virtue.

When we decide to make changes in our lives, we are in control as the ultimate agents of the change that we hope to see. If we believe that our spiritual lives are the function of changes that we can make by adhering to certain rules and behaviors, we have not surrendered to God's transforming work, which can happen only when we relinquish control.

We have all had experiences, in the Enneagram and beyond, of being so sure after we read a particular book or attended an inspiring conference that our lives would never be the same again. We would surely make the changes that we had journaled about. A new list of steps or dos and don'ts would equip us to lay claim to our best lives. Until we didn't. *We forgot.* We never picked the journal back up again. Our lives returned to normal, but a few months later we restarted the process when the next book got recommended to us and the new conference bill was posted.

Disappointment in our progress is always the result when we try to take charge of our lives. We make changes and they last until they don't. We commit to resolutions until we forget that we've made them. We all have books on our shelves that we were sure were going to change our lives, and when we look at them now, we think, *I remember that I really liked that book, I should read it again!*

The processes of change and transformation are different. Change usually involves taking something new on, and transformation usually involves allowing something old to fall away so that something older can be rediscovered. Transformation lasts longer than change. Transformation reorients us in such a significant way that we often look at life as before and after. Whereas change—which can be wonderful and can bring some great, lasting results—requires maintenance and constant feeding to keep on course.

Change and transformation are cousins to one another, and we can't always dissect the fruit of our lives to determine which label best applies. Many times, change leads to transformation. A diet that you faithfully adhere to for years becomes a lifestyle, and you don't have to remind yourself to eat a certain way any longer—you just do. Similarly, people who have found success through the recovery movement can attest to the demanding work that they have undertaken to make significant changes in their lives. But many of the people who work the recovery steps for an extended period will tell you that they feel truly transformed—while at the same time acknowledging the fact that they are always working toward the change, which takes commitment.

The reason I describe the Enneagram and contemplation as transformation tools is because I don't think we can do anything lasting with them from a posture of willfulness. A willful posture to life places us in charge as the agents of our own destinies. In contrast, a willingness approach to life postures us to both receive new gifts and surrender things that no longer help us. From an openhanded willingness stance, we are ready for God's great undertakings in our journey toward soul growth. You cannot *will* yourself to become spiritually or mentally healthy. Spiritual growth and the expansion of our souls is something that happens to us. Our work is to open ourselves to God's working in us, which happens through contemplation.

Until we learn to let go, we will never find our true selves. The words can get in the way, but try on and test my approach: we are responsible for the growth of our souls and not for anything else in the spiritual realm. God has taken care of all the heavens and hells, and God has already called us beloved sons and daughters despite our recognition or lack thereof.

The way that we promote soul growth is through a spiritual posture of letting go, not taking on. And contemplation is fundamentally a posture of letting go rather than taking on. As we lean into the spiritual posture of contemplation, we will naturally—without any of our willful doing—see our false self grow smaller and our true self grow larger.

We are invited on the sacred journey of letting go to find ourselves—the truest selves that have always been the most intrinsic part of us but which we have masked and ultimately forgotten about as we have been building our personalities—as expressed in our Enneagram types—year after year, decade after decade.

Breaking the cycle does not require more willful doing. You don't have to learn anything new or build any new habits. Instead, you must unlearn all the unhelpful adaptations and projections that have covered up who you truly are. You must let go to find you.

One of the defining features of the historical Enneagram is that Enneagram teachers rarely taught the tool without including a companion faith tradition. The combination of personality system and spiritual wisdom tool is what compels me to the Enneagram. Other personality-typing systems are wonderful and have great insights to teach us as we become healthier individuals living in flourishing relationship to self, God, and others. But the defining feature of the Enneagram that keeps me coming back for more is its unification of personality system and spiritual tradition. This unification is necessary if real transformation is going to happen. The Enneagram does not work as a quick fix to live your best life now. The Enneagram does not give us a clear set of steps to follow to become healthier people. The Enneagram instead offers us insight through spiritual tradition. We are not our personalities; we are more than just our Enneagram numbers. We are souls; we are essences; we are our true selves. And the Enneagram is only useful in so much as it helps reveal and rediscover our true self.

One of my spiritual heroes is Henri Nouwen. He was a Catholic spiritual teacher and priest who also happened to be an Enneagram 2, like me. Because of our mutual connection of Enneagram number, I feel a particular resonance and kinship to Nouwen's life and work. Through his small book *In the Name of Jesus*, Nouwen has provided one of the best guides to distinguish between the true self and the false self by writing about a transition in his vocational life from status to significance.[3]

Much of Nouwen's professional career was spent in service to Ivy League institutions, where he taught religion and spirituality at the highest levels. As a lecturer at Harvard and Yale, and a speaker on some of the grandest stages around the world, Nouwen was in demand for his spiritual teaching. Toward the end of his life, he had the opportunity to make a change. People wondered where his next teaching post would be, what his next best-selling book would include, and where his exciting travels would take him. But Nouwen surprised many of his followers by choosing to move to Canada, where he became the spiritual director at L'Arche Daybreak, a residential community for adults with cognitive disabilities.

Nouwen wrote *In the Name of Jesus* as a testament to some of his struggles in making the transition from the Ivy League to seeming obscurity. He wrote that the questions that people asked him revealed the most notable distinctions between his life at Harvard and his life at L'Arche. He wrote that the most important questions he received when he worked in the Ivy League were about his upcoming accomplishments. But once he moved to L'Arche, the most important question he received daily was a quite different and much simpler one: *Will you be home in time for dinner?* The community members he lived among and served at L'Arche were uninterested in his prizes and résumé and more interested in his presence. Nouwen wrote that his shift in perception forced him to deal with the distinction *between his relevant self and his unadorned self.*

His relevant self, according to Nouwen, was the self that he had spent his career building. Relevant self was the self that could do things, build things, prove things, and accomplish things. Much of his life and work had been in service to building his relevant self. His unadorned self, however, was the self capable of giving and receiving love apart from any accomplishments. The relevant self was the self that the world invited Nouwen to grow, and as his relevant self grew, his unadorned self became increasingly hidden beneath the layers of his accomplishments and prizes.

Relevant self is another way of describing our Enneagram type. The Enneagram describes nine different relevant selves. Nine ways of proving things, building things, accomplishing things, and doing things. But behind and beyond these nine relevant selves are nine styles of unadorned self. These unadorned selves can give and receive love apart from any accomplishments. Our Enneagram passion is an articulation of relevant self, and our Enneagram virtue is an articulation of unadorned self. Relevant self is the territory of Enneagram number, and unadorned self is the realm of the soul.

It was not until Nouwen left elite institutions and moved to seeming obscurity that he was able to see his relevant self, or his Enneagram number's passion, fall away so that his unadorned self—best articulated by his virtue—could reemerge from years of hiding.

Nouwen's journey illustrates the work of transformation. Old things must pass away so that new things may emerge, but the new thing is really the oldest thing of all: our soul's dormant virtue, hiding behind a lifetime of building a relevant self through the passion of our Enneagram number.

More than one gospel writer offers us the words of Jesus telling us that whoever seeks to save their life will lose it and whoever seeks to lose their life will find it. These words of Jesus reflect the fundamental distinction between change and transformation.

One of the temptations for many earnest students of the Enneagram is to accumulate as much Enneagram knowledge as possible in hopes that something will stick and make the changes they are seeking in their lives. From knowing your number to triads, stances, orientation to time, centers of intelligence, passions, virtues, fixations, holy ideas, subtypes, tritypes, and all sorts of other Enneagram buzz words that fill books and social media feeds, there can be a temptation to gobble up more and more and more. Spirituality can provide similar temptations—to read as many books as possible, listen to as many podcasts as possible—all in hopes that the accumulation of information will bring about the changes that we hope to see.

But in both the spiritual life and Enneagram wisdom, less can be, and often is, more. The striving and accumulating of Enneagram wisdom and spiritual insight is nothing more than adding layers to our personalities as we continue to remain in charge while we undertake change in our lives. We need transformation, not change. We need the transformation that involves letting go and opening up rather than holding on and grabbing more. In the spirituality of subtraction, as we have less clutter (*physical and metaphorical*) in our lives, we remove distractions that keep us from an inward journey.

Even good things like Enneagram study and spiritual devotion can become distractions from the simple work of letting go. In my Enneagram teaching, I encourage people not to adopt the belief that they must become experts in all available Enneagram knowledge. If you employ the wisdom of the Enneagram as a lifelong spiritual discipline, then there will be opportunity for you, across the years, to mine the assorted topics that have been written about and studied in the Enneagram school. But if all you ever do is learn your core number and understand a few things about it—like the distinction between your number's passion and virtue, which we will turn to next in this book—you have enough to set you on a journey of transformation that will reacquaint you with the divine living inside of you.

Letting Go, Finding You is simple because we need simple. *I need simple.* And I am guessing that you do too. Change is hard, but transformation is simple. Be assured that transformation will not be quick or free from suffering, but fortunately, our path to transformation is uncomplicated.

When Jesus said, in Matthew 18:3, that unless we become like little children, we will never enter the kingdom of heaven, he revealed to us that entering the kingdom of heaven—whatever we imagine the kingdom to be—is so simple that even children can do it. As adults, we like complicated solutions because they feed our sense of control. But becoming like a child means shedding the layers of false self that have accumulated through the years and rediscovering our true selves that were present before we did anything wrong and before we did anything right.

We must become like little children and shed the false path of forging our own way, making our tremendous change, and adopting discipline after discipline. If we want to truly find the joy and purpose of aligning our lives with God and the deepest iterations of our souls, then simple is what it will take.

3

True Self vs. False Self

What We Miss When We Focus Only on the Passions

The passions, some of the earliest discovered seeds for the modern Enneagram of personality, were first recognized and named by Evagrius Ponticus, who described nine ruling temptations that block us from our deepest fulfillment. Pope Gregory I refined the passions down to seven, which we have come to know culturally as the seven deadly sins. The nine Enneagram passions restore fear and deceit to the seven deadly sins, returning us to Ponticus's original nine.

The Enneagram passions are sometimes recharacterized, under the historical influence of Pope Gregory I, as sins. In modern life, we have a complicated relationship with the concept of sin. Some of us grew up in nurturing spiritual environments that emphasized grace and inclusion, while others of us grew up in spiritual environments that focused on how sin can keep us out of heaven. For that reason, I rely on the traditional Enneagram characterization of passions rather than on sins. But regardless of the language that we use, the nine passions represent the behavioral adaptation that most blocks each Enneagram number from achieving wholeness and fulfillment.

Much attention in Enneagram teaching and literature is given to the passions. If you have attended any introductory, or Know Your Number, workshop, you have likely encountered teaching about the Enneagram passions. Less attention, however, has been given to the Enneagram virtues.

The nine Enneagram virtues are articulations of our best selves. Oscar Ichazo, a twentieth-century spiritual wisdom teacher based in Chile, is credited with bringing the modern version of the Enneagram of Personality to the United States in the 1970s and with first describing the nine virtues of the Enneagram. It makes all kinds of sense to me, and is in keeping with a primary message of this book, that for over fifteen hundred years, we were wrestling with and describing the bad news—*the passions*—before we took the time to develop a language for the good news—*the virtues*. Once Ichazo's language of virtues formed, Enneagram teachers began to see that even though it took us a lot longer to name the virtues than it did the passions, the virtues came first. So much of our humanity continues to be wrapped up in the troubling awareness that it is so much easier to discover and describe what is wrong with us than what is right. We began talking about our personalities, our false selves, our passions, before we ever had a language for what those personalities, false selves, and passions were protecting. A deficiency in Enneagram teaching, including much of my own, is that teachers often share the bad news without also sharing the good news. We focus on the problems and the neuroses of the nine Enneagram types. But we give less attention to the beautiful parts of each Enneagram type, particularly the virtues.

The passions and the virtues are one discipline. Teachers and authors should not bifurcate the passions and virtues but should describe them together as one unified idea. The passion for each number is the opposite of the virtue for that number, and the virtue is the opposite of the passion. They are paradoxes of one another.

The passion for 1s is anger, while their virtue is serenity.
The passion for 2s is pride, while their virtue is humility.
The passion for 3s is deceit, while their virtue is truthfulness.
The passion for 4s is envy, while their virtue is equanimity.
The passion for 5s is greed, while their virtue is nonattachment.
The passion for 6s is fear, while their virtue is courage.
The passion for 7s is gluttony, while their virtue is sobriety.
The passion for 8s is lust, while their virtue is innocence.
The passion for 9s is sloth, while their virtue is action.

Once we recognize that the passions and the virtues are opposites of one another, we must look deeper into their relationship. We can reconnect the passions and the virtues by describing the passion as the articulation of our small self, our false self, our personality, or our Enneagram type, and the virtue as the articulation of our larger self, our true self, our essence, or our soul.

The virtue associated with our Enneagram type is the truest articulation of the God-image that each of us bears. *Virtue is the real thing.* Furthermore, we enter the world as infants most connected to our virtue. However, our early lived experiences and the school of hard knocks requires us to protect our precious virtue. If our virtue is unprotected in our early years of life, we feel too exposed. In response to our need to protect our vulnerable, precious, God-indwelling virtue, we mask our virtue by projecting its opposite, which is the passion.

We come to be known by the passion that is associated with our Enneagram number, just as we come to be known by our personality. But the truer thing that could be said about each one of us is that our passion and our personality is an adaptive, protective reaction to our early awareness that the world is too filled with peril to wear our virtue on our sleeves. The virtue associated with each of our Enneagram types truly embodies our essence.

The passions are not the final story about us. In fact, your passion is the opposite or the counterfeit of who you truly are. You are your virtue, not your passion.

In ways that go beyond the Enneagram discipline of passions and virtues, your Enneagram type is an articulation of the opposite of who you truly are, which is why Enneagram wisdom teachers use the language of the true self and the false self. The false self is not false because it is bad; it is false because it is the counterfeit of the true.

Several years ago, I had the opportunity to travel to Kalamazoo, Michigan, with Suzanne Stabile, who was teaching the Enneagram at the Fetzer Institute and a nearby spiritual community called Transformations. One of our hosts for the weekend was a nun named Sister Betsy, who lived at a convent near our teaching site. Suzanne and I were immediately drawn to Sister Betsy's generous spirit and humor. We sensed that she was a person who had been formed through a lifetime of service and contemplative spiritual practices.

After several days of teaching, Suzanne and I had a few hours before leaving for the airport, and Sister Betsy asked us what we would like to do. We both agreed that we wanted to tour the convent with her. She took us to the beautiful, sprawling campus of the Congregation of Saint Joseph. The campus was everything you could imagine a one-hundred-year-old convent would be.

Sister Betsy led us through the long and winding hallways filled with religious artifacts and spiritual icons. We could easily imagine how St. Joseph's beautiful campus had provided such a significant spiritual home and formation center for all the nuns who had lived there. We saw dormitories, offices, community gathering rooms, and courtyards, but the real showstopper came as Sister Betsy led us into the chapel. As she guided us through, she informed us that the entire campus was slated for demolition in just a few months. Suzanne and I were horrified. How could anyone want to tear down such a beautiful campus that provided a nurturing center of mission and home for nuns? But Sister Betsy explained that her community of sisters had grown so small, and many were so advanced in age, that it was no longer practical to continue their work and support their large campus.

The chapel at Saint Joseph is stunning. The room smelled and looked like a great cathedral of Europe, with its stone floors and walls, stained glass windows, ornate and intricate wooden carvings, and pews that had clearly supported generations of souls as they met daily for spiritual practice. As I took the room in, I noticed that there was a common visual representation that thematically tied the entire room together. On the side of each pew, on the pulpit, and on the Communion table was a carving of a bird. I was not sure what the bird was, but its striking appearance drew my attention and caused me to ask Sister Betsy to explain its meaning to me.

Sister Betsy smiled and said, "Well, that's a peacock, Hunter!"

A peacock? I was familiar with depictions of peacocks with their tail feathers spread out in a beautiful fan, but this peacock's tail was closed and draping the ground. Sister Betsy told me that in spiritual tradition, the peacock with his feathers down is a representation of humility, while the peacock with his feathers puffed out is a representation of pride.

Through Sister Betsy's explanation, I began to understand how St. Joseph's humble group of nuns could face the demolition of their home and way of life with gratitude and resilience. I am an Enneagram 2, which is the number commonly recognized through its caricature of being helpful, cheerful, giving, altruistic, and sensitive. We often call Enneagram 2s the Helper or the Giver. When I began to discover Enneagram wisdom, I learned that the traditional passion associated with Enneagram 2s is pride. At first, I was turned off by hearing that my passion was pride. I thought that I had surely misheard. But I learned that Enneagram 2s exhibit the passion of pride as they elevate themselves to the position of the helper rather than the helped. The savior rather than the saved. The fixer rather than the fixed. And unfortunately, these descriptions fit me to a tee.

Our pride as Enneagram 2s is that we underrecognize and underacknowledge our own weaknesses and needs, which is a rejection of our own broken humanity. Most days, I want everyone to see me as strong and capable—when, really, I have the same or greater needs and fears as all the people whom I am trying to help. I had no idea how much I needed to learn from Sister Betsy and the architectural wisdom of the chapel at Saint Joseph. *Of course*, I did not recognize the bird with its feathers brushing the ground as a peacock! I am overacquainted with the pride of self-deference and underacquainted with the humility of self-acknowledgment.

For many of us on our Enneagram journeys, the story starts with passion. We learn the bad news before we learn the good news. But the real story—the truest story—is one of good news. One of hope, blessing, and virtue.

Many of us who began our spiritual journeys in conservative Christianity learned about sin before we learned about blessing. We missed the beginning of the story and jumped right into the fall of humankind and the introduction of sin and perceptions of separation from God.

In my experience of Christian evangelicalism, the Bible begins at Genesis 3 rather than Genesis 1. We begin with sin, separation, problems, heartache. All leading us toward the story of Jesus, who brings reunification, restoration, and healing. But the Bible does not start in sin; the story starts in blessing. The good news comes before the bad.

The authors of the Hebrew Bible chose to tell the story of the beginning of all things with God speaking creation into existence. Creation was pure, beautiful, and perfect. God spoke light and land and creatures into existence. And God blessed everything. All was a gift; everything was perfect and true. God called it good. Nothing was missing; nothing was corrupted.

A couple of chapters into the story, the authors introduce a new character—a deceptive serpent that supposedly tricks the first man and woman into thinking that what they have isn't enough—that they could have even more of a perfect thing, becoming like God—if they snatched up more of the perfect gift than was theirs to take. Once the man and woman buy into the serpent's deception, greater understanding comes, and they become aware of and ashamed of their nakedness, hiding from God. The whole story takes its turn and the ideas that we know of as sin, separation, fallenness, and curse enter the story. But the story did not begin there. The story began in blessing. The story began in goodness.

In the same way, our personal stories do not begin in sin, separation, or curse. Our stories begin with good news.

Blessing before sin.
Virtue before passion.

We carry out the virtues of God in our innermost beings from the time we are born. We forget them at some point along the way, and our invitation is to recover, rediscover, and remember who we truly are. And so, before we go deeper into exploring the nine passions of the Enneagram, let's center ourselves in the virtues. Some of us have become so lost in our personalities and the strategies for survival that they falsely promise us that the virtues will seem strange and unfamiliar.

To carry out the image and likeness of God is to carry out God's essential nature—God's attributes or character. In the New Testament, the fruit of the Spirit is an articulation of God's essential attributes. In the letter to the church at Corinth, attributed to the apostle Paul, faith, hope, and love are the core eternal attributes of God, with the greatest being love (1 Corinthians 13:13 NIV). God is love. God is virtue. If God is everything that is true, beautiful, and good . . . if God is full of and dripping over with love, then the nine virtues are certainly descriptions of God's eternal nature. Albeit imperfect descriptions, since no words can capture the mysteries of the universe. The nine virtues described by Enneagram wisdom are true, eternal things. They are the qualities of God. And so, when we bear out and carry these virtues inside of us, we are living out our fundamental calling as creatures made in God's likeness.

To be made in the image of God is no small assertion. I am not sure that we feel like we are God bearers very often. Most of the time, I am more aware of my weaknesses than I am of my strengths. At the trust company in Nashville that I currently help lead, I recently asked our management team to compile an analysis of their strengths and weaknesses in preparation for an annual management retreat. Each member of the management team submitted their written assessment of personal strengths and weaknesses to me ahead of one-on-one discussions that we had in anticipation of the team-wide discussion at our retreat. To a person, everyone gave much greater attention to their weaknesses than their strengths. Several people had three or four bullet points for perceived strengths, while pages of prose were devoted to opportunities for improvement and perceived weaknesses.

In *Hardwiring Happiness*,[1] psychologist and author Rick Hanson provides a helpful analogy: in the face of praise, we act like Teflon, and in the company of criticism, we act like Velcro. Criticism sticks to us, while praise falls off. Many of us have work to do in acknowledging our bearing out of God's image and likeness. The fundamental attributes of God are inside each one of us, whether acknowledged or not. We are usually slower to see the seeds of love, goodness, patience, and faithfulness in ourselves than in others—or to trust when others see those attributes in us. It will take us a lifetime of spiritual awakening, of falling down and getting back up again, to believe that we are God's image bearers, but we are!

One of the nine virtues is our feature virtue. It is the doorway or entry point that leads us into the room of virtue, where we find the other eight living within us as well. One of the virtues is most connected to our Enneagram type and is our pathway to rediscovering the truth about who we really are. If we can recover the one virtue that is most particularly ours, our primary virtue will lead the way for us to embrace a self-awareness of the good news of the Enneagram—that we are blessing, not curse; virtue, not passion; true self, not false self.

One reason that Enneagram teachers do not often begin by telling people their virtue is because doing so would make it far more difficult for anyone to learn their Enneagram type at our workshops. Sadly, one reality of being human is that we know ourselves better by what we get wrong than by what we get right. If I spend hours telling people all the "bad news" about each Enneagram type, it's likely that listeners will walk away knowing which

Enneagram number best describes them. If, on the other hand, I spend hours talking about the gifts, God image, and virtue for each Enneagram type, listeners might enjoy the positive descriptions, but the success rate for identifying Enneagram numbers would plummet.

The curse of understanding our stories better through the lens of Genesis 3's sin and separation means that we have work to do to see ourselves through the lens of Genesis 1's blessing and perfection. Fortunately for us, our work is not hard; it's simple. Our work will not be another list of dos and don'ts. Our work will be a return to a simple way of practicing our spirituality—a contemplative journey. But more about that later.

The nine Enneagram virtues are greater than the words that describe them. But words are what we have, and so words are what we turn to. Just know as we explore each of the nine Enneagram virtues that these words are mine. You know yourself much better than I do. When, through your new contemplative practice, you leave the room of false self and passion for the room of true self and virtue, you will discover better words than mine to describe the virtues, *yes, plural*, that live inside you.

Enneagram 1s: Rediscovering Serenity

The feature virtue for 1s is serenity. Serenity is full and total nonjudgmental acceptance and allowing of everything the way it is. Full-blooded acceptance rejects judgment or criticism. Serenity includes an awareness of objective and observable failures, yet still sees the good. Serenity is not naivete or closing our eyes to what is wrong, but serenity grounds us in the present reality that all things are whole and complete as they are.

The dualistic mind characterizes Enneagram 1s, who naturally sort things into categories: right or wrong, like or dislike, done well or not finished. Enneagram 1s struggle to accept things as they are—especially themselves. They have an inner critic that tells them constantly how they could self-improve. Enneagram 1s "should" on themselves and others regularly by their negative feedback toward self and others and by their continual striving to perfect themselves and the world around them.

You can see how serenity is the antidote for striving in Enneagram 1s. From a place of serenity, Enneagram 1s can accept themselves for how they really are: the imperfect, unfinished, yet completely whole and accepted person made in the image and likeness of God.

In 2017, I had the chance to teach the Enneagram in several evening sessions on the Christian music singer Amy Grant's cruise to Alaska. My final evening session focused on spiritual practices that can be helpful for each Enneagram number. I told the attendees that they should focus on the practices for their own number, making some notes, and simply listen to the practices for the other eight types.

My mother, who had come on the cruise to support my early teaching venture, found a place near the front of the room. My mother is an Enneagram 1, which is where I began the session. Then I moved along and taught the remaining eight numbers. My mother took notes all through my practices for Enneagram 1s, seeming to write down every word I spoke. But then I noticed as I moved on to teaching the other numbers that she was still taking copious notes. She filled page after page with the spiritual practices that I described for each Enneagram type.

During a break, I walked over to my mother and said, "Gosh, Mom, you seem to be taking really great notes!"

She smiled and said, "Well, I heard you tell us to only take notes on our own Enneagram type, but then I thought to myself, 'Wouldn't it be better if I could master the spiritual practices for all nine numbers, and not just the practices for Enneagram 1s?!'"

Enneagram 1s, like my mother, are working so hard to be right and to do right that they end up being hard on themselves and on the people they love. Their virtue of serenity is the solution to their uncompromising drive. Serenity invites Enneagram 1s to embrace the beautiful wholeness of what is. Through a recovery of their core virtue of serenity, Enneagram 1s can stop taking inventory of themselves and the world through the dualistic lens of good and bad and can instead see that everything belongs.

My mother loves to go to a little place that she has on Lake Cumberland in Bronston, Kentucky. She is a nature lover at heart, and nothing makes her happier than walking the roads inside Woodson Bend Resort and counting the deer that she sees. When she escapes her busy life in Nashville for a weekend at the lake, she sends me pictures of all the flowers, creepy-crawlies, and deer she discovered during her walks and golf cart rides. At Woodson Bend, my mother can finally leave behind the narratives of responsibility, duty, and expectation that are so difficult for her, as an Enneagram 1, to escape in the routines of ordinary living. Some of the freest expressions of joy and the deepest conversations that we have had have been spent in the rugged natural beauty of south-central Kentucky.

My mother's weekend pilgrimages to her simple brown cedar, Berber carpet, screen-porched home at the lake are journeys to serenity—toward the center of what is truest about herself. Her walks through the woods are where the mind's clutter finally escapes and the passion of anger recedes.

The serenity that my mother finds counting the Lake Cumberland deer reminds her that she is both fully complete and in progress. Nothing is missing. No more striving is necessary for her to be accepted by God and by those whom she loves.

In my Enneagram teaching, I counsel Enneagram 1s to regularly schedule travel from their daily routines to escape the responsibilities that loom so large in their minds. This travel doesn't have to be expensive or long. A four-hour drive to a country antique store and back will do. These miniature escapes are ways of practicing a more serene way of living, and as Enneagram 1s experience serenity and detach from anger more and more, the pathway becomes clearer and the opportunities to touch serenity and deflect anger, like trained muscles, become easier to adopt in the ordinary and routine.

Serenity is a beautiful inner peacefulness that cannot be diminished by the world of shoulds and oughts, musts and coulds.

Enneagram 2s: Rediscovering Humility

The feature virtue for Enneagram 2s is humility. In our time and culture, we often think of humility as the laying down of trophies and accomplishments, but for Enneagram 2s, humility invokes the laying down of our need to be set apart. Humility for Enneagram 2s is not putting yourself down; it is embracing the mutuality that comes from seeing yourself not as set apart but as *set beside* everyone else in your life. You are no better and no worse than all the people whom you love.

What Enneagram 2s want are places of significance in the lives of others and in the communities that they are a part of. Enneagram 2s long for love, acceptance, and belonging, but their drive to be set apart means that while others may admire and honor them, they do not belong in the ways that they deeply desire to belong. Enneagram 2s often put themselves in the seat of the fixer, the helper, the savior, so that they can avoid being in the seat of the fixed, the helped, or the saved. As the children's song goes, "It's not my brother, not my sister, but it's me, O Lord, standing in the need of prayer."

This past Thanksgiving, my aunt Carol brought an exercise for our family to do together after dinner. Aunt Carol is an education professor at Eastern Kentucky University, and the exercise was developed by one of her student teachers for the semester. Each participant starts with a list of thirty personal values, such as integrity, honesty, humor, cooperation, and perseverance. The facilitator leads participants through a clarifying experience of eliminating values, five at a time, until what remains is each participant's five most important core values.

So, while our turkey settled in our stomachs and the pies baked, Aunt Carol gathered our little family by the fireplace outside and walked us through the values exercise together. It was frustrating for each of us to have to keep eliminating values that were important to get to our final five core values. The Enneagram 1s in our group especially struggled to cross off words like *honesty* from their pages to get to their final five. At the end of the exercise, each person shared their final five and we each got a deeper insight into each other as no one around our fire had the same top five core values. When my turn to share came, I started with my first remaining core personal value on my page: *recognition*. Recognition did not show up in anyone else's top five and I was embarrassed that it showed up in mine. But my most honest inventory had me admitting—to myself and to my family—that recognition is more important to me than values like honesty, integrity, and cooperation.

As Enneagram 2s, our cultivation of recognition and set-apartness is as altruistic as it is a coping strategy to avoid the inner work of exploring and naming our feelings, needs, and fears to another person. If 2s can be the helper rather than the helped, we can see ourselves as strong, capable, independent, worthy, and good. But as soon as we admit our need for help and reveal our "sameness" to someone else, we lose our place of otherness, and the pedestal slips from beneath our feet.

In May of 2020, I was diagnosed with multiple sclerosis (MS). In the fall of 2019, I began experiencing numbness in my legs, along with several other symptoms that were easier to ignore at the time. Before my MS diagnosis, doctors encouraged me toward physical therapy in the belief that I had a herniated disc in my back. But when my symptoms didn't improve and after a week in February of 2020 when it was nearly impossible for me to walk (I had stood on a makeshift milk crate stage for eight hours one Saturday teaching the Enneagram in a church basement), four MRIs and a spinal tap confirmed my diagnosis of MS.

I was scared. It has only been in the last ten years or so that effective drugs have been developed to slow MS progression, and so my experiences of the disease were limited to several people I knew who were of my parents' generation and had been in wheelchairs for most of their adult lives. Immediately after diagnosis, I began a five-day steroid infusion treatment to try to get some of my symptoms, like numbness, drop foot, and lack of balance under control. I felt terrible for those five days and many days afterward. I couldn't continue to be the happy helper and martyring self-sacrificer that had fed my ego and defined my personality for thirty-five years. Suddenly, I couldn't stand as long as I used to. I couldn't do the things for others that I had prided myself in previously. Friends and family showed up in big ways—bringing fresh-baked bread, helping me with my work, taking some of my responsibilities from me, and writing me notes of the kindest encouragement. I felt like I had come to the end of myself as most of my abilities to serve and help others were temporarily taken from me. The tables had turned, and I didn't like it.

My forced experiment in humility, arising from my MS diagnosis, felt humiliating. I wasn't practiced in slowing down, letting go, paying attention, accepting help from others, quieting my body and mind, or any of the other things that a newly onset chronic condition demands.

But MS was the gift that I needed most to help me learn who I truly am. My journey from pride to rediscovery of humility was propelled by the literal humiliating experience of stumbling down stairs, catching my foot on every carpet, and dropping my drink as my fingers grew numb. You may be recoiling at my language of gift when describing MS, but it is honestly how I experience it. The physical pain and existential frustration that MS brings me is also accompanied by gratitude for a chronic disease that teaches me to slow down, depend on others, and savor each moment that I feel well. In my early days of MS diagnosis and treatment, I adopted a mantra: *It's a good day to have a good day.* Any day that I feel mostly well and can physically do all the things that I want to do is a good day to have a good day. None of us knows how many of the "good" days we have left.

I don't resonate with battle metaphors, and I think much of the Christian faith has been perverted by a false commission of our own making that we are soldiers in God's army.

And so I don't feel very connected to any sort of language that suggests that I am "fighting" against MS or "winning" any battles. *How can I become well if I'm fighting against my body?* My MS represents both my heartbreak and my best spiritual teacher. I am learning lessons in my thirties that most people don't have the opportunity to learn until their sixties or seventies as their bodies stop performing to demand.

Rediscovery of humility came for me in disguise of an enemy. But as I have learned to embrace my whole self—the sick parts of me and the well parts of me—I have been better able to rediscover my truest self: the humility implanted deep inside, carrying the image of the divine in me. A humility that was tucked and covered and buried away as long as I could come to every rescue. Until finally I couldn't. *Letting go, finding me.*

The great truth and mystery for Enneagram 2s is that we will never find the love and belonging that we so desperately want until we rediscover the great gift of humility—a humility that is most particularly ours as Enneagram 2s—and find our place *in* the story rather than in front of or above the story. Humility is the great gift of Enneagram 2s. Humility is the virtue in us that most beautifully and completely bears out the image and likeness of God.

Enneagram 3s: Rediscovering Truthfulness

The feature virtue for Enneagram 3s is truthfulness, sometimes described by an older word: *veracity*. Enneagram 3s often feel beat up by Enneagram teachers who describe 3s as being so driven by the need to succeed and accomplish that they will shape-shift their identity into whatever they need to become to be the successful prize winner. These descriptions can make Enneagram 3s sound duplicitous and dishonest. Enneagram 3s are not trying to deceive the rest of us through their contextualizing and shapeshifting; they are deceiving themselves. Enneagram 3s have so lost touch with their own true self that they believe they are each of the identities that they embrace in their journey to success.

The virtue of truthfulness for Enneagram 3s is an invitation to discern and discover who they truly are. Truthfulness, as the virtue for Enneagram 3s, is a commitment to discern and commit to a core identity of who they truly are and to let that commitment be their North Star for the decisions that they make in their life. Truthfulness for Enneagram 3s is less about *saying* true things and more about *embodying* true things. Until Enneagram 3s rediscover and return to their core virtue of truthfulness, they will shift themselves and adapt to whatever their current context defines as success—losing more of themselves along the way.

My friend Laura, who works with me in Life in the Trinity Ministry, is an Enneagram 3. Laura lives in Asheville, North Carolina, and has a wonderful job in youth ministry at a church—a job that she is so well-suited for in experience, her seminary training, and in her innermost person. Before moving to Asheville, Laura lived in Dallas and worked in youth ministry at a large church there. When Laura's husband, Tate, got a job offer in Asheville that was too good to pass up, they decided to move, which meant that Laura had to temporarily leave her career behind. When she arrived in Asheville, she started looking for work but struggled to find a perfect job that combined her passion, experience, and training.

Laura found work as an administrative assistant for a women's inpatient counseling facility in Asheville. As an Enneagram 3, she poured herself into her new work and made fast friends with her new colleagues. Laura enjoyed the job and, after working there for six months, came home one evening and told Tate over dinner that she had decided that she wanted to go back to school to get a master's in counseling. Tate, who of course knew Laura well, was initially surprised since he knew that Laura had loved her work in youth ministry in Dallas and he thought that finding a new youth ministry role in Asheville was still Laura's main goal. He listened sensitively and asked Laura several exploratory questions. By the end of their dinner conversation, Laura had discovered that she did not want to go back to school or pursue a master's degree and that she did not even want to remain long-term at the company where she currently worked. Laura, who had been doing work for years with the Enneagram and other spiritual tools, was able to admit to Tate by the end of dinner that, as an Enneagram 3, she had identified the steps necessary for her to advance in her work and that was driving her decision. It took an open conversation with her partner to arrive at the realization that the deepest truth about her vocational aspirations meant returning to youth ministry. Laura is now serving her local church in Asheville as one of its youth ministers and she is fully alive doing it.

Enneagram 3s are great at nearly everything they put their hands to, but only when they put their energy into activities most aligned with their deepest sense of self and personal values will Enneagram 3s become fully alive. And the world needs more people who are fully alive—committed to truthfully carrying out their inner light in the ways that are truest for them.

Enneagram 4s: Rediscovering Equanimity

Enneagram 4s are a special number, so they get a special word for their feature virtue: *equanimity*. In Enneagram wisdom, equanimity is the balancing of all things with a spirit of composure and evenness in temper.

Enneagram 4s are prone to swings in affect and mood. Emotions are dynamic, not static, for Enneagram 4s. Think back on all the emotions you have experienced over the course of the last two weeks. There were days of happiness, days of loneliness, days of contentment, and days of disappointment. The strange and surprising news is that Enneagram 4s experience that same spectrum of emotions in twenty minutes. The ability to dynamically experience the full range of emotions in a brief period feels like both a blessing and a curse to Enneagram 4s. The blessing is their connectivity to a full experience of life and the ease with which they can empathize with anyone. The curse is the feeling that Enneagram 4s do not control their emotions but their emotions control them.

Equanimity is temperance of emotion, not emotionlessness. The goal for Enneagram 4s is not to cut out emotion and get to a place of flat or low affect; the goal is to bring balance and temperance to their playing out of the emotional experience so that complex, dynamic emotion does not keep them from taking action and living the life that they want to live.

Another truth hidden in the Enneagram 4's virtue of equanimity is the completion or balancing of all things. Without tools and work, an underlying misease that something is missing haunts Enneagram 4s—as they search for what is missing in them, in their partners, in their families, in their work, in their home, *in everything*. Enneagram 4s can become addicted to the perpetual quest for the elusive thing that will finally bring completion.

The virtue of equanimity provides the antidote to their perpetual quest by bringing awareness of the completeness, or fulfillment, of all things. Of course, things could always be better. Of course, we all have wishes and hopes for how we could change our lives, change our bodies, change our careers, and change our partners, but the continued pursuit of what *could be* means willfully ignoring the wonderfulness of what is. The temperance, balance, and satisfied completeness that equanimity brings to an Enneagram 4 offers the promise of contentment.

In my family, we have a beloved saint—my great-grandmother whom we called TeeTone, a nickname coined by a child in the church preschool—who lived to be 103. Today, two decades after her death, our family holds her memory as a guide and stay. Like all saints, her edges have worn off and all that remains is the glow of her good qualities, her humor, her resilience, her faithfulness. Each Thanksgiving, I remember her 101st Thanksgiving, when we gathered around my aunt's table in Kentucky. The family sat together at the table filled with days' worth of southern cooking. There had to have been ten or fifteen side dishes spread among the fatted turkey and ham. We sat down to our feast and held hands for the blessing. We began filling our plates; even with just a spoonful of each option, they still overflowed. After everyone had their plates and we settled joyfully into the occasion, TeeTone surveyed her plate and lifted her head to say, "If I just had a dollop of coleslaw, all of this would be perfect." No one reacted, but I imagine the thought response of everyone who had spent days cooking our feast would have been something like, *Well, did you bring the coleslaw?!* And while TeeTone was not likely an Enneagram 4, her surveying of the feast only to notice what was missing will resonate with all Enneagram 4s.

In my Enneagram seminars, I often describe the Hebrew Bible's Joseph as the patron saint for Enneagram 4s. And because there are several interesting Joseph figures through the Christian Scriptures, I remind people that I am describing Andrew Lloyd Webber's Joseph: *Joseph and the Amazing Technicolor Dreamcoat* Joseph! (Forgive me, but like all good gay kids, I forever love Broadway musicals.)

When we first meet Joseph in the stories of Genesis, he's a special kid with a special mom and some really special gifts. He can interpret dreams and he has visions that seem to his father as verging on prophetic. And so, just to demonstrate how special Joseph is, his father commissions a special coat for him—one that is brightly colored and far outshines the drab ornaments that the rest of his brothers wear in their sheepherding careers.

Joseph's brothers hate him. To them, he is pompous and self-celebrating, and they endeavor to remove this special brother from their midst. His brothers scheme together a way to rid the family of their multicolored-coat prophet, setting off a long journey of hard knocks for Joseph, from slavery to jail.

Toward the end of Joseph's story, his luck has reversed. He has been selected by Pharaoh to be a trusted and decorated adviser, all while the luck of his brothers has run out. Genesis describes a dramatic scene where Joseph's brothers come to grovel for food at the feet of Pharaoh's assistant (not recognizing who the assistant actually is—their brother).

Finally, Joseph's moment for vengeance is nigh. He has the opportunity—as an elevated leader in the land—to exact the revenge that he surely must have been plotting against his murderous brothers for his decades of slavery and incarceration. But somewhere along the journey, Joseph entered a wisdom journey. Joseph discovered who he truly was, and he had long abandoned any scheme for revenge or gotchas.

Instead, Joseph—like all virtue-bearing Enneagram 4s—removes himself from his pedestal of grievance, authority, and superiority and decides to belong rather than be set apart. He rejoins his family. He forgives. He lays down his specialness and embraces the ordinary beauty of tempered emotion and familial belonging. Joseph is the redeemed Enneagram 4 of the Bible. He, like all Enneagram 4s, had incredible gifts and abilities that had all the potential to set him apart from everyone else, in every way. But Joseph found his true strength and his true giftedness when he laid down his specialness and joined the common story.

Without returning to their core virtue of equanimity—the part of God's likeness and image most central to the Enneagram 4—Enneagram 4s will always survey the feast of living before them and find that the abundance comes up short. If you are uncomfortable in the even-tempered emotions—as many Enneagram 4s are—you will always be searching for emotions and experiences that are extraordinary. But when they find their way back to their core virtue of equanimity, Enneagram 4s can access the even-tempered, ordinary emotions that rest balanced in the center of the emotional spectrum between elation and despair.

Enneagram 5s: Rediscovering Nonattachment

The feature virtue for Enneagram 5s is nonattachment. Nonattachment is a different state of being from detachment altogether. Nonattachment is the ability to hold all things loosely. If the posture for detachment is hands outstretched with palms out to push away the world, the posture for nonattachment is hands extended with palms facing up—the posture of both giving and receiving.

Enneagram 5s are great at detaching. Detaching, for this type, often involves pulling away from relationships or withdrawing from the outer life toward a hiding in the inner life. For Enneagram 5s, their detachment can be obvious or subtle. Sometimes you cannot find them and you sense that they have ghosted you. In other encounters, they are physically present, but they find a way to be miles away relationally whether you notice or not. My friend Ben, an Enneagram 5, tells me that whenever he attends a party with a lot of people whom he does not know, he finds a chair to plant himself in. From his little detached oasis amid the hoopla, he can observe and casually participate when he wants to, but he is able to lose himself in his thoughts and limit his engagement if needed.

Enneagram 5s have many attachments, both to physical objects and immaterial things. They can attach to financial resources, like Ebenezer Scrooge from *A Christmas Carol*, fearful that if they spend or give anything away, they might run out of that. They can attach to physical items in their homes, finding comfort and security in belongings or supplies. But they attach to their time and their energy as well. Enneagram 5s believe that their time is their own. If you would like to have some of it, you can petition them for it, but no promises that the time will be granted! Similarly, they treat their energy like the Israelites treated manna in the wilderness during their exodus story as told in the Hebrew Scriptures—just enough for the day. Enneagram 5s carefully plan and measure out how much energy can be devoted to each person and task that pops up during their day. And so, they may skip the meeting or let the phone call go to voicemail when they feel like they are running low on their energy reserve.

All these attachments to time, energy, money, resources, and more, for Enneagram 5s, come from a place of scarcity, not abundance. The wounding message for Enneagram 5s, as delivered to us by Don Richard Riso and Russ Hudson in *The Wisdom of the Enneagram*, tells them not to be too comfortable in the world because resources are scarce, so they better learn to hoard, ration, and preserve what they have to make sure that they don't run out.[2]

The virtue of nonattachment comes from a mindset of abundance, not scarcity. Nonattachment means that you hold all your resources—your time, your energy, your affection, your material resources—with open hands, ready to use them, spend them, and give them when needed, trusting that more is available and that you will have what you need when you need it.

Enneagram 5s have a greater capacity for nonattachment than all the other eight Enneagram types because nonattachment is their core virtue. It is the great gift hidden within. And so the lifetime of work for Enneagram 5s involves recovery of their precious virtue by casting off a scarcity mentality and reengaging with an abundance mentality. Nonattachment rather than attachment or detachment. Openhandedness rather than tight, closed fists.

My friend Kenny is a pastor in my hometown of Nashville. An Enneagram 5, Kenny is a great preacher and an even better thinker. He is one of the most well-read people I know. Kenny has shared that his struggle with preaching is that Sundays are like telephone poles on the highway. As soon as you pass one of them, the next one comes right up. He said that as he is preparing every sermon, he reaches a point where he panics. His panic-reducing strategy is to go to his Amazon app and order a book, on next-day delivery, related to the subject of his sermon. Never mind that he has filled his office and his mind with books on every subject under the sun. In his momentary panic during his weekly sermon preparation, he turns to additional resources to counteract his perception of his lack of knowledge.

Returning to the virtue of nonattachment for Kenny allows him to draw from the deep well of experience and wisdom that he has accumulated in his sixty years of living. He does not need to fill up with more. He needs to open his mind, his heart, and his hands to allow the accumulated wisdom of his life's experiences and his diligent study to flow out into the sermons that are already inside of him—taken from years of life and study, not from the latest book.

In August of 2021, the church in Nashville where Kenny served as associate rector experienced a terrible tragedy. The church's fifty-year-old senior rector died in an interstate car accident with his child while he was driving his child to college for the semester. Kenny was unenviably named interim senior rector and selected by fate to be counselor and first griever to a stunned congregation while also sorting through the loss of one of his best friends.

There is nothing that you can purchase on Amazon that can accurately prepare you to walk in the shoes that Kenny was forced to walk in during this season of life. No book that he could find would have helped. His life was the teacher that he needed. The wisdom and grace of over fifty years of living are what prepared him to help a grieving congregation through their shared loss. Only through letting go and adopting the virtue of nonattachment could Kenny's true wisdom, gained from a lifetime of living, loving, and serving, shine.

Suzanne Stabile has a teaching that will be familiar to all her students. The teaching is based on the story of Jonah. In her beautiful, storytelling way, she mines four mantras as she recounts the story of the boy who winds up in a whale's belly while on his way to Nineveh: show up; pay attention; tell the truth; and don't get attached to the results. Enneagram 5s, in their passion, have the hardest time not attaching themselves to the results of their actions. *Will I have enough? Will it work? Will I run out? Will I be shown to be incompetent or unable or unwilling?* Only through their precious virtue of nonattachment can Enneagram 5s remain unattached to the results. And when they finally reach this posture of nonattachment, they begin to truly live.

Nonattachment for Enneagram 5s is a beautiful way to live. Nonattachment is generous and full, always trusting in the goodness and abundance of all things. When

Enneagram 5s live from a posture of nonattachment rather than attachment or detachment, they recover the rich, precious virtue inside that holds all things in a faithful and generous looseness. For those who seek to save their lives will lose them, but those who lose their lives for the sake of others will find them.

Enneagram 6s: Rediscovering Courage

The traditional feature virtue associated with Enneagram 6s is courage, but I want to offer a reframing by calling the virtue faith. Courage, to me, seems like something that we muster up in the face of fear and problems. But faith—one of God's gifts that remains forever, according to the apostle Paul—is something that we embrace and receive rather than something that we will ourselves toward. Faith is a gift. Faith is an offering. For Enneagram 6s, faith is an openhanded holding, with palms out and turned up, ready to receive and ready to give. Enneagram 6s are vigilant, prepared, and ready. They anticipate problems and accumulate solutions so that they are ready for whatever trouble comes next—regardless of how likely or unlikely.

When I was young, my aunt Carol had the warmest and most welcoming house, on Beresford Avenue in Lexington, Kentucky. I loved going to her house as a child. As soon as I walked through the door, the scent of sugar cookie candles and beef stroganoff in the crock pot enticed me in. Aunt Carol's house was a split-level house—popularized in the 1970s—sort of a "choose your own adventure" layout where as you entered the front door and stood on the shallow landing, you were offered an immediate choice of whether to ascend or descend. At the top of Aunt Carol's stairs was a large antique trunk that lined up perfectly with the front door. As you ascended the staircase and landed at the top step, you had to shift to the left to avoid kicking its base.

I never saw inside the trunk or even thought much about it. But years after Aunt Carol moved into a different house, we would still reminisce about the house on Beresford. During one of those conversations, I recalled the antique trunk at the top of the staircase and asked Aunt Carol about it. She told me that inside of that trunk were all the precious family things, such as photos, mementos, and heirlooms, collected across her lifetime. She went on to tell me that the placement of the trunk was strategic, so that if there had ever been a housefire all she had to do on her way down the stairs and out the front door was to give that antique trunk a swift, strong kick and the trunk would *kerplunk* its way down the staircase and shoot out the front door, saving all of the precious family memories. Enneagram 6s plan with Aunt Carol's vigilance for every eventuality. Their gift and their curse is a hyperawareness of all that could go wrong.

And of course, there *can* be housefires and unexpected tragic events. When the worst things happen, the rest of us are so grateful for the Enneagram 6s in our lives, who were preparing while the rest of us were blissfully unaware of the dangers looming round each bend.

My friend Phil is a musician in Nashville and an Enneagram 6. When I first met him, he was hired by the church that I would later pastor to be staff arranger—writing, orchestrating, and arranging all the scores that the choir would sing in Sunday services and record for its albums. He is a delightful human all around and embodies more than anyone I know the true-to-the-core goodness that characterizes Enneagram 6s.

As Phil's life in Nashville grew and evolved, he had more and more opportunities to do freelance arranging for choral projects produced by Christian music publishers across the city and even won a Dove Award, the Christian music equivalent of a Grammy. All musicians know how risky the full-time freelance gig is, and Phil, especially being an Enneagram 6, appreciated the predictable paycheck that came month by month from the church for his services. But as I came to know and love Phil, I watched his journey evolve to a place where the job at the church just didn't fit any longer. It no longer provided him with the time or the launchpad that he needed to continue to build his personal career in the music industry. For Enneagram 6s, leaving a predictable paycheck to follow their North Star toward the career of their dreams, full of financial risk and question, is harder than it would be for nearly every Enneagram type.

Fortunately, Phil has been on the wisdom journey, and the work of contemplation, Enneagram wisdom, and inner life gradually formed him into a wisdom person. He was able to overcome his fear of failure to courageously pursue the career that he was so clearly destined to take on. We smiled and celebrated on Phil's last day at the church, knowing that he was continuing down the courageous wisdom journey toward hard days and good days—but all days tied to bearing out his truest self as a risk-taker, an encourager, a freelance musician, and a great friend.

Enneagram 6s can find comfort in knowing that their virtue of faith tethers them to something greater beyond themselves. The revealing that, as Julian of Norwich still reminds us, all will be well—all manner of things will be well.

According to John's Gospel (in John 16:33 NIV), Jesus promised that we would have trouble. *And don't Enneagram 6s know it!* They are not wrong in their anticipation of, accounting for, and planning around trouble. Danger, worries, and problems are all around us. But the second part of Jesus's promise is the summation of the Enneagram 6s' invitation to reclaim their precious virtue of faith: "Take heart, for I have overcome and am overcoming the world." The virtue of faith is not naivete. Faith is not blind, head-in-the-sand avoidance of the gravities and realities of our modern world. Even in the face of trouble all around, as people—albeit doubters still—rooted to a spiritual story of belonging that is bigger than our time and space, the virtue of faith offers the promise of a peace that passeth understanding.

Enneagram 7s: Rediscovering Sobriety

The feature virtue for Enneagram 7s is sobriety. In our culture, sobriety has come to mean a lifestyle of abstention from drugs or alcohol for those who previously had expressed addictive behaviors toward such substances. But sobriety, in Enneagram understanding, means several things: *The ability to find joy in everyday or mundane circumstances. The capacity to savor the little things. The embracing of a both-and approach to emotional well-being—if deep sadness does not belong, then neither does the pinnacle of joy.* And while in our culture, sobriety usually means a full, teetotaling abstinence, abstinence is not the goal. Instead, Enneagram 7s can embrace sobriety through moderation. The Enneagram invites us all to balance and specifically invites Enneagram 7s to savor experiences in a moderated way.

I love Broadway musicals. My grandfather was a theater director at a small college in Kentucky, and some of my earliest memories are being picked up from school on Friday afternoon by my parents and driving from Nashville to Campbellsville, to make the opening night curtain for one of my grandfather's musicals. These early experiences inspired in me a love for acting and theater. My favorite date night activity still involves watching a local play or musical.

Several years ago, I had the opportunity to travel to New York City for a long weekend to see a couple of Broadway shows. One of the shows that I experienced that weekend was *Pippin*—a musical I had never seen before. *Pippin* is a coming-of-age story about a boy looking for meaning and belonging. As the boy becomes a man, he embarks on a quest to discover the ultimate source of meaning by trying out many of the classic places where we, as humans, look outside of ourselves to find significance. He tries power; then he tries love; then he tries great wealth; and on and on.

Pippin has the insight of an Enneagram 7 who has followed the passion of gluttony as far as he can follow it. For an Enneagram 7, and for Pippin, when you get to the end of the buffet line and you have tasted everything that life has to offer, you can either turn toward despair that the options, which previously seemed endless, have run out or you can embrace the wisdom journey of turning toward savoring rather than tasting. Deeper rather than wider. Simple joys rather than excess fascinations. Pippin's arc is a beautiful and fairy-tale–like depiction of the wisdom journey for this number. The passion of gluttony—born from the Enneagram 7s' wound and the resulting suffering—is a lifelong trap that can keep Enneagram 7s from finding joy and satisfaction in the simple pleasures of nature, self-reflection, love, and friendship.

For each of us, no matter our Enneagram numbers, the passion is a trap that is set to catch us over and over again. If we do not find ways to embrace the wisdom journey, we'll step into the trap every day and, like Pippin, move from episode to episode always searching for more but never finding enough. Thich Nhat Hanh is a Buddhist author who has a beautiful series of little "how to" books, including *How to Relax*, *How to Sit*, *How to Eat*, and *How to Love*. In his book *How to Eat*, he describes eating an orange. He describes the color of the orange. The bumpy, glossy texture of the rind. The initial burst of sweet citrus scent when your fingernail pierces the rind and begins to peel the outermost layer away, revealing the wet, sinewy fruit beneath. An orange is a delight that has the capacity to fill each one of our senses. The virtue of sobriety offers us an invitation for something as divinely simple as eating an orange to awaken all our senses and connect us to the goodness of God.[3]

Yesterday, as I was mapping out a few thoughts for this section of the book on a Post-it note, I wanted some sort of distraction, so I walked downstairs from my office to the kitchen and found the drawer of leftover Halloween candy. I pulled out one of the fun-sized packets of M&M's. I could feel that the packet had only eight to nine pieces in it, so I peeled back one side of the package and turned the whole thing upside down into my mouth. My experience with the M&M's lasted about fifteen seconds. And—as you may have guessed—it was not particularly satisfying.

But here's another story that illustrates the true value of sobriety—ironically, it is a story about bourbon! One of the great gifts of the last ten years of my life has been gathering regularly with a book club. One of my friends whom I met while I was a student at New York University, Daniel, started a modest monthly gathering in the basement of his house for an eclectic assortment of his friends—none of whom knew each other—with the goal that each month, we would read and discuss a new book and try a new bourbon. From Wendell Berry to Warren Buffett, we read books that we would have never discovered and tasted more bourbons than I knew existed. As I am writing these words, just this month, we celebrated ten years of monthly gatherings. And as most groups who stick together across long stretches of time, the friendships have become about so much more than books and bourbon. On our ten-year-anniversary night we sat on Daniel's screened-in porch and celebrated the love that we have shared over the past decade.

A couple of years ago, my father, who has become an amateur bourbon collector, gifted me a bottle of Pappy Van Winkle bourbon. For the teetotalers among us, Pappy Van Winkle is one of the rarest and hardest bottles to get your hands on. If they have the chance to buy one, people will spend thousands of dollars and display the bottle proudly among their collection. When I received the gift, I was grateful, but the bottle sat sealed up on my shelf for years. There never seemed to be an occasion worthy of opening it. But when the ten-year anniversary of my book and bourbon club came near, I discovered the right moment to bring out the Pappy.

The eleven of us gathered around, smiling, and each lifted our glass with a half-ounce pour of Pappy Van Winkle in celebration of our decade of living and loving. We lifted our glasses, inhaling the notes of oak and vanilla. We took the smallest drop on our tongues and savored the rare flavor. We spent fifteen minutes or so relishing each drop of the half-ounce pour. This was our way to enjoy the Pappy. This was our way to celebrate our decade together. This was our way to savor our love.

Sobriety offers meaning and contentment beyond the thrill of a moment. From stuffing our mouths to savoring small bites.

Enneagram 8s: Rediscovering Innocence

Innocence is the feature virtue for Enneagram 8s, which can be a challenging virtue to explain and to desire. I find that when I first describe the virtue for Enneagram 8s, I am met with skepticism. Is innocence really a virtue? many wonder. Innocence sounds like a naive virtue to desire in a world as harsh as ours.

In many ways, Enneagram 8s lost their innocence earlier than the rest of us. I do not mean to suggest that they started exhibiting immoral or risky behavior earlier. What I mean is that earlier than the rest of us, they learned that not everyone's motives are meant for your good—even, and sometimes especially, the people who are supposed to love you the most. From an early age, Enneagram 8s are keenly aware that everybody in their life can betray them. So, they learn to become tough, strong, and independent. They protect themselves from vulnerability so that people both near and close to them are not in possession of information about them that could be used to hurt or betray them.

Enneagram 8s are invited to recover the virtue that lives closest to their core—innocence. The difficulty is that they often see their strength, tenacity, toughness, and independence as their superpower. They can be slow to see the ways in which their emotional distance from others has kept them from the love and belonging they truly desire.

As I have mentioned previously, one of the central tenets of living in the *Rule of St. Benedict* that becomes a mantra is *always a beginner*. Benedictine spirituality encourages bringing a beginner's mind to all things and abandoning expert status. For Enneagram 8s, the offering of a Benedictine way of living involves an expectation of surprise. Enneagram 8s are rarely surprised. They expect to get what they got. They are students of people and systems, and they do not expect to experience something different from a person or a system than what they experienced in the past. Enneagram 8s adopt a sense of expert status, especially of people, which is often expressed through cynicism toward or skepticism of the motivations of people around them. But when we expect to get what we got before, these expectations and patterned responses can become self-fulfilling prophesies.

The Benedictine emphasis on always being a beginner can lead Enneagram 8s back toward their virtue of innocence by allowing each moment, each experience, and each interaction to stand on its own—free of fairly or unfairly preconceived judgments. When Enneagram 8s can stand in beginner posture toward the people and experiences near to them, they open themselves up to the possibility of being surprised, and the ability to experience childlike surprise is one of the great gifts of life.

Inner child work can be a great offering to Enneagram 8s if they will suspend their disbelief long enough to try it. Inner child work can lead this number to reengage with the child within before all the boundaries and emotional walls were erected to try to keep people from betraying their vulnerable tenderness.

In the first year-long cohort program that I coteach from the Micah Center in Dallas, we had an attorney from Texas named Jeff. Jeff was an Enneagram 8's 8. Not only was he an 8, but he was also a trial attorney who had mastered the art of defending his clients and capturing the attention of both judges and juries through the intensity and mental toughness that he brought to his law practice. I admit that when I first met Jeff, his presence intimidated me. Big in stature, he also brought a military-like command to any room he was in. But our group quickly discovered that he—like many Enneagram 8s—was a teddy bear encapsulated in a bristling exterior.

During our third-quarter gathering that year, we arrived back in Dallas on a hot Thursday afternoon. Jeff arrived in flip-flops and took his usual seat in the front row. Before the gathering began, my coleader, Rev. Joe Stabile, noticed and could not help but point out that Jeff's toes, displayed prominently in his flip-flops, were painted pink. We had come to know and love Jeff well over the past year and we knew that pink toes were off-brand for him. If I had arrived with pink toenails, no one would have likely thought much about it, but for Jeff, we had to ask!

"Jeff, your toenails!" Joe exclaimed.

Jeff smiled and told us the story of his pink toes. He is divorced and gets to spend time with his daughters several weekends during the month. As his daughters entered their tween years, he had to think of new ways for them to enjoy time together on his custody weekends. He shared that he had recently begun a ritual of taking his daughters to get pedicures on Saturday mornings. After several trips to the salon—where he sat beside and talked with his daughters but did not participate in the ritual of pampering—his daughters convinced him to join the fun and get a pedicure too.

Jeff agreed but told the nail technician to skip the polish. He said that as he finished his first pedicure, which felt amazing, he wondered why he had waited so long to allow his feet to be pampered. After a few more months of salon visits, his daughters finally wore him down to allow some polish to be applied to his toes. He let his youngest daughter pick the color. And so, this is how burly Enneagram 8 Jeff arrived at the Micah Center with painted toenails.

Without meaning to, Jeff had found his way back to the virtue of innocence. His love for his daughters and his desire to connect deeply with them led him to shed the emotional boundaries and walls that had been bricked in for years to join his daughters in the joy of painted toenails. And the virtue had so resurrected within him that he showed up to the Micah Center in flip-flops rather than in socks and shoes. He was so taken by the childlike innocence that he experienced with his daughters that he wanted to share the joy with the rest of us too. We smiled and laughed together, and we understood.

Enneagram 9s: Rediscovering Action

The feature virtue for Enneagram 9s is action, better described as "right action." We can unfortunately caricature

Enneagram 9s as lazy, but that is an unfair assessment. Enneagram 9s are usually busy—in fact, they can be some of the busiest people along the Enneagram spectrum. However, they are often busy doing other things to avoid getting to the hard things they know really need to get done. Action on its own is not a virtue for Enneagram 9s, but *right action* is.

One of the primary motivational drivers for Enneagram 9s is the desire to be at peace—from within and without. They wish they could skate through life unaffected by conflict. They defer or delay many of their own dreams and ambitions because pursuing those dreams means potential conflict. To really understand what conflict means for Enneagram 9s, we must expand our connotations to include self-assertion as a major potential source for conflict. When I think about conflict, as an Enneagram 2, I think about tense dialogue, fighting, or misunderstandings between another person and me. But when an Enneagram 9 thinks about conflict, they think about all of that plus the inner conflict that arises when they stand up for themselves, pursue their own dreams, and offer themselves to the world. Because of their underlying wounding message, which falsely leads them to believe that their presence might not make that big of a difference, any form of self-assertion can create an inner conflict where their desire to act comes up against their self-doubt as to whether their action will really make a difference or whether people will bend to accommodate them.

When other numbers feel that Enneagram 9s are being lazy or have gone to sleep to life, withdrawing from the rest of us, it is usually due to Enneagram 9s' inner conflict between their desire to act and their uncertainty about the meaningfulness of their presence.

Recently, I was taking a trip with my partner, Bradley, an Enneagram 9. We had bought our airline tickets from Southwest at separate times, so they were not on one reservation, and when we checked in, his boarding position was A42 and mine was C13. When boarding started, Bradley lined up with the A boarding group and I told him to save me a seat since the plane would be nearly full by the time the gate agent called the C group. When I finally got on the plane thirty minutes later, he was sweating and looked like a deer caught in the headlights. As soon as I sat down, he told me, "We're never doing this again. I am never saving a seat for you again!"

The stress for Bradley, an Enneagram 9, of having to tell dozens of people as they tried to sit down in the seat beside him that he was saving it for someone boarding later had stolen all his peace for the day. While our airplane experience may seem like a silly example for many people, Enneagram 9s will understand!

Right action is the precious virtue that lives at the core of each Enneagram 9. Right action is not about being busy or getting daily tasks accomplished. Right action is about committing yourself to tackle and finish the four or five things throughout your lifetime that are meaningful imperatives. The virtue of right action invites Enneagram 9s to take action that may create conflict inside of them or between them and another person—but action that they know is critical for them to take to be faithful to themselves and to their calling.

It is difficult for me to think of a better example of the lived-out virtue of right action than my friend and mentor, Rev. Joe Stabile. His life is a living example of right action. He is a cradle Catholic and sensed a vocation to ministry from an early age. At the age of thirteen, he left home and entered a Catholic seminary preparation school. He followed his emerging vocation all the way to the priesthood in the order of St. Vincent de Paul, serving in various church leadership positions throughout Texas.

By the age of forty, Joe had given twenty-seven years of his life to preparation for and service within the Catholic Church. But along the way, he had had a spiritual awakening that led him to begin questioning some of the beliefs and practices within the Catholic Church, especially around the role of women and laity in ministry positions. His theology and understanding were expanding beyond the borders of traditional Catholic doctrine, and an inner conflict continued to grow inside of him as he tried to balance the vows he had made in his ordination and his evolving sense of Spirit-led movement toward what he believed to be fundamentally true.

So, Joe made the decision, at the age of forty, to leave the Catholic priesthood. His decision meant leaving a career, family, friendships, financial security, and in the unkind estimations of much of his community, God. As Joe made his final decision to be faithful to his sense of where God was leading him, his former employer—the

Roman Catholic Church—sent him on with two thousand dollars, an instruction to buy clothes that were not black, and a final requirement to sign a paper acknowledging that in the eyes of the church, his life was destined for hell.

How else could a cradle Catholic, loyal friend, and Enneagram 9 make such a life-altering choice that alienated him from nearly all his loved ones than through resurrection of the virtue of right action? Joe's decision was costly in every way imaginable, yet he walked into his next season of life unwaveringly because he knew the action he was taking aligned with his own inner compass and his private sense of God's calling. *Right action.* Again, right action for Enneagram 9s is doing the handful of things across a lifetime that you fundamentally know you are called to do—no matter the cost; no matter the heartache; no matter the conflict.

To get to right action often requires eliminating the distracted actions that keep your inner voice quieted. If we stop long enough—and not by numbing activities such as Netflix binges or social media scrolling—to listen to our inner witness that reminds us of our deepest callings and desires, we will know what right action to take. The question is, Will we be faithful to take it? Not because God requires our action or because we will be damned if we don't but because our inner knower requires it. In my Enneagram teaching, I often remind Enneagram 9s that the absence of conflict does not mean the presence of peace. The pursuit of true, lasting peace often requires us, like Joe, to risk conflict with ourselves and everyone that we have loved to be faithful to what we know is fundamentally right and true for us.

Jump In!

Everyone who has had the experience of immersion in water—whether pool, pond, lake, or ocean—knows that there are generally two ways that you can enter. The safest, *but let me just tell you, also the most painful*, is to enter the water inch by inch, step by step, little by little. It seems like the easiest way to enter, but it means that until you finally cover your chest in water, your body is going to be in a continual adjustment mindset. Until your chest is surrounded by water, you feel each rising inch of cold water covering your body.

The other way to immerse yourself in water is to jump in. It seems like the riskiest way because, in the flash of a second rather than little by little, your whole body will experience the cold plunge. There is no getting adjusted when you jump in. You go from totally dry to totally wet in an instant. But unless you are swimming in a cold-water plunge, when your body resurfaces, bursting through the ceiling of water, your temperature is at once adjusted to the temperature of the water and everything feels great. It's scarier to enter the water this way, but it's the quickest and easiest way to cut down how much time you are aware of the water's coldness.

When we begin our wisdom work, whether through the Enneagram and contemplation, as this book suggests, or through the myriad other entrance points that one can enter the wisdom journey, reacquaintance with our virtue hidden deep within seems to happen like the first water immersion process I just described—little by little, step by step, inch by inch. We practice taking off our passion and letting our virtue shine through. It seems easier this way.

As an Enneagram 2, as I have reacquainted with the virtue of humility it has felt easier in fits and starts. I've become thoughtful of my intention to try on truth-telling about myself, acceptance of help from others, and intentional diminishment of my drive to make myself into the hero of the story.

Like a child visiting the ocean, sometimes I feel that first burst of cold around my ankles in my fear of self-exposure and loss of control, and I turn back and run as quickly as I can back to the familiar, dry sand. But as I put more years into the wisdom work—not through any mastery of steps or perfect fulfillment of self-determination—I have learned that if I jump in, my life is so much easier. As opportunities to practice humility arise, and I yield fully to them, the pain of letting go of my passion of pride becomes easier and easier.

Our schoolteachers encouraged us that practice makes perfect and there's something to that in the spiritual life as well. There is no perfect in the spiritual life, but as we practice letting go of our passion and surrendering to our virtue, the work of transformation in us becomes more habitual and patterned. We can jump into virtue quicker and more easily than we used to.

The hope is that over time, we catch ourselves living in virtue more than just experimenting with or practicing virtue.

For 1s, *living* in virtue looks like serenity at home, not just on vacation.

For 2s, *living* in virtue looks like humility in accepting help from the people whom you feel the most responsible for, not just the stranger.

For 3s, *living* in virtue looks like truthfulness in commitment to your most personal passions, not just in work that contributes to your professional success.

For 4s, *living* in virtue looks like equanimity in the biggest opportunities for emotional swings, not just in more regulated days.

For 5s, *living* in virtue looks like nonattachment to the things that you deem most crucial to your survival, not just the things that are more readily replaced.

For 6s, *living* in virtue looks like courage in trusting your own inner guidance, not just in expecting plan A to work.

For 7s, *living* in virtue looks like sobriety in emotion, through allowing yourself to sit in pain long enough for it to have its journey in you, not just slowing down and savoring a simple experience.

For 8s, *living* in virtue looks like innocence that makes one vulnerable to betrayal, not just the cherishing of an inner child's experience.

For 9s, *living* in virtue looks like action that demands self-assertion, not just activity.

Life is a sequence of falling down and getting back up again, all the way home. Letting go of passions so that we can rediscover our virtues represents our lifetime of spiritual work. We will be submitting and resubmitting to this work of God's transformation in us until our final breath. We strive for continual growth and evolution rather than perfection. Living, dying, and rising—all the way home.

Like Mister Rogers in *A Beautiful Day in the Neighborhood*, our hope is that what we can mention, we can manage. You have the language now for your virtue. You have the understanding now that your passion—which represents the opposite spirit from your virtue—has developed over time as an adaptation that once seemed helpful, but now is smothering. And with this awareness, you have the tools to better manage your habitual, patterned responses to life's events that lead us into the same messy and exhausting predicaments, time and time again. *What we can mention, we can manage.*

May it be for me, and may it be for you.

4

Twisting the Truth

How the Virtues Became Passions

It does not take long for each one of us to encounter interpersonal harm in life. Part of the human experience is to misunderstand one another and treat each other worse than we meant to. From our earliest days, we learn to hide who we truly are so that we can become more acceptable to people whose praise and attention we want. We hide the truest parts of ourselves because those are the parts that we cannot bear to present to an unaccepting world.

And if our sacred virtue is an articulation of what is most precious and true about us, it's no wonder that our virtue is what we learn to protect. Just like a child protects their precious treasure in a box hidden beneath their bed, we protect the most sacred parts of ourselves from the possibility of rejection. Our innermost robings happen so early in our lives and so naturally that we are not explicitly aware of the adaptations going on inside of us. Like most coping strategies and adaptations that we make during our lifetimes, the work is done subconsciously, outside of our ordinary, specific awareness.

In the face of our ever-growing awareness and estimation of the world's judgments against us, we hide. We adapt. We evolve. We change. We project. And the mystery revealed by the language of the Enneagram is that we project the exact opposite of what is true. As people most prone by their innermost gifts to the virtue of sobriety, Enneagram 7s project gluttony. As people most prone by their innermost gifts to the virtue of humility, Enneagram 2s project pride. And as people most prone by their innermost gifts to the virtue of truthfulness, Enneagram 3s project deceit.

The mystery that I am describing, which is truly hiding in plain sight, first became apparent for me when I noticed that the passions and the virtues were opposites of one another. For some of the Enneagram types, our traditional connotations of the words reveal the paradox in the passion and virtue clearly, as in pride and humility for 2s, deceit and truthfulness for 3s, fear and courage for 6s, gluttony and sobriety for 7s, and sloth and right action for 9s. The other Enneagram types carry the same paradox, or opposite, in their passions and virtues, but we must work a little harder to understand how the words capturing the passions and virtues for the numbers are opposites. Anger and serenity for 1s, envy and equanimity for 4s, greed and nonattachment for 5s, lust and innocence for 8s. The important thing to take in is the paradoxical relationship between each Enneagram type's passion and virtue.

The truest thing about each one of us is the opposite of what our personalities project. You are the opposite of who you have come to know yourself to be and who you are known to be by others. But until our habitual and personality-based patterns of behaving and responding run out of steam and stop working so well for us, we are not ready to embrace the good news that we are the opposite of who we seem to be. But after we've relied one too many times on strategies that continue to produce the same unsatisfactory results, we're ready to go deeper and find the parts of ourselves—the precious virtues—that lie dormant and hidden beneath our personalities.

The paradoxical relationship between the passions and the virtues is why the dichotomy of true self-false self is so often employed in Enneagram literature and teaching. In my first several years working with the Enneagram, I ignored the distinction between true self and false self because the words did not resonate with me. My understanding of the word *false* carried a negative moral evaluation. How could I call my personality—which is (in its best moments) helpful, altruistic, sacrificing, and kind—false? The language of personality as false self felt wrong to me. Labeling some of my most treasured behaviors as articulations of a false self felt like a rejection of what I believed were the best parts of me. Slowly, I came to understand the false self-true self dichotomy differently.

Let false mean the opposite of true. False, in the language of the Enneagram, does not carry any moral weight. False does not mean bad. False does not mean evil. False does not even mean untrue. (Please bear with my semantics here.) False means the opposite of true. For instance, as an Enneagram 2, I am sometimes extraordinarily helpful and kind, self-sacrificing and demurring. Those aspects of my personality can be born from a place of my passion or my virtue. I can self-sacrifice in a way that is honest, authentic, and true—from a deep place of humility—desiring to truly offer love without expectations to someone that I care deeply about. But I can also self-sacrifice in a way that is twisted—connected to my passion of pride—when I give with the expectation of receiving something (usually place, status, or recognition) in return.

The language of the Enneagram describes what motivates us more than how we act. The behaviors for Enneagram numbers can be remarkably similar, but the motivations are distinct and different. For example, Enneagram 2s and Enneagram 7s can act in optimistic, positive ways that resemble one another closely. But the motivating drivers behind the actions of Enneagram 2s and Enneagram 7s are quite different. Enneagram 2s are motivated by a need to be needed and a wounding message from childhood that directs them to push down their own needs and promote the needs of other people as a strategy to find love and belonging. Enneagram 7s, on the other hand, are motivated by a need to be self-sufficient and self-reliant, informed by a wounding message from childhood that tells them not to depend on anybody for anything.

Our actions, habitual ways of responding, and behaviors are not necessarily false, but our motivations can be. Each Enneagram number's actions can look the same whether they emerge from a place of virtue or from a place of passion, but the underlying motivations are different. The distinction between our true selves and our false selves that the wisdom of the Enneagram can offer us is that deep down, we are not what we seem to be. And the distinction between false self and true self can only be good news to those of us who have grown tired of our personalities.

Before we turn to the how-tos and how-dos, we need to confront the honest differences between our actions when they are motivated by our passions rather than our virtues, through a deeper exploration of the nine Enneagram passions and how they emerge as opposite, paradoxical projections of the nine Enneagram virtues that they protect. A fundamental truth of living is that when we act on behalf of our false self, we act to disguise our true self.

Enneagram 1s: From Serenity to Anger

Enneagram 1s, whose feature virtue is serenity, learn from an early age to protect their precious virtue from being exposed by disguising serenity with its opposite: anger.

Anger is their passion and motivates them to continually strive, improve, and perfect themselves and others. Anger, which is primarily directed toward self, keeps them dissatisfied with what is and always orienting toward making things better, most especially themselves.

A more specific word for the anger that drives Enneagram 1s to act is *resentment* because resentment is anger born from the heart. Built-up anger in the heart is not always externalized but can lay dormant or hidden for a long time. But the resentment that Enneagram 1s feel toward others for the ways they have let them down by not following the rules or doing their part is always present and, at some point, will bubble up and expose itself as externalized anger. This number's expressions of anger are often outsized or misdirected because the anger has been accumulating.

In my Enneagram seminars, I sometimes play-act the resentment that Enneagram 1s feel through monologue:

> I've spent my whole life doing things the way they are supposed to be done. By keeping to all the rules. Doing things the way we all agreed they should be done. But, somewhere along the way you must have stopped believing that the rules applied to you, because you started to do your own thing. You started to have fun. You started to leave your part undone. And you leaving your part undone meant that I had to do my part and your part. But don't you think I wanted to have fun too? Sure, I would have loved to let my hair down and throw caution

> to the wind. But somebody had to do the work. Somebody had to do what must be done. Somebody had to be dependable.

Can you hear the resentment in my fictional Enneagram 1's heart?

Enneagram 1s become so accustomed to acting from their motivating passion of anger that they come to depend on anger to provide them with fueling energy. They befriend the anger and stop believing it is a block to their own happiness or to flourishing relationships with others. Instead, they believe their anger, whether self-directed or externalized, is their superpower. It's the juice that keeps them going. It's the flow that keeps them moving. It's the drive that keeps them perfecting. And all the while, they neglect to own their anger, often shouting (at least in our estimation), "I'm never angry; I'm just disappointed," or "I'm trying to help us all to be better."

It is true that Enneagram 1s accomplish a lot and that they are good at getting things done. If an Enneagram 1 tells you that they are going to do something, you do not have to check in to see whether they will follow through or not, but the underlying—often hidden—anger that undergirds their action leaves a trail of pain in their wake.

What if, instead of being motivated by anger, all the productivity and accomplishments of Enneagram 1s could come from a place of serenity—their core virtue? Recovering serenity over anger does not have to mean the Enneagram 1 loses their lofty standards or perfecting touch, but energy born from a place of inner peace and serenity doesn't leave a path of destruction behind them.

My friend Rebecca has a son in high school. For years, she got up each morning and packed his lunch for school, making the perfect well-balanced lunch as only an Enneagram 1 could. One day, Rebecca had a couple of important things that she had to finish in the morning at home before leaving for work, so she told her son that he needed to pack his lunch for school. She came down the stairs and into the kitchen just as he was cramming his homemade sandwich, which was already falling apart and oozing condiments from every side, into a Ziplock bag. Without any time to censor herself, she shared her reaction: "Oh, that's how *yoooouuu* make a sandwich?"

Rebecca's son grinned, clearly proud of his self-sufficiency, and replied, "That's right!" And he scurried off to meet the bus in time. Rebecca, who has been on the wisdom journey for a long time, decided that the pride that she saw in her son's eyes over his messy sandwich was worth more than her need to make him the perfect lunch every day, so she began a practice of asking him each morning if he would like to pack his lunch for himself. If he says yes, she stands back and watches him make his lunch in ways that couldn't be further from her ways. But through the simple smile of serenity, Rebecca is practicing giving up her need for perfection. She is celebrating her son's messy participation in his lunchbox preparations; as she does so, without even knowing it, she is practicing letting go of anger, which motivates all her perfecting, and reacquainting herself with serenity, which builds with every grip on perfecting control that she surrenders.

But before Enneagram 1s can transform, they must want to change. They must open their eyes to what their anger is costing them, which is mostly inner peace and relationships. They must admit the ways their anger has kept them from being good to themselves and the people they love the most. The world is filled with people who recognize the things that are wrong in their lives but will not give them up for something better because they believe that to give them up would mean sacrificing their end goal or destination. But productivity and action birthed from serenity rather than anger can have the same successful results without all the collateral damage in relationships that anger brings.

And so, the invitation for Enneagram 1s is to look within and ask what their anger has cost them. And with a faithful self-inventory, they can make a commitment to transformation. A commitment to leave the false self and its angry motivations for the true self and its serene peace.

Enneagram 2s: From Humility to Pride

Pride is the passion for Enneagram 2s. If they begin life with the full capacity to express their virtue of humility, somewhere along the way, they learn that loved ones will not meet or honor all their expressed needs. It is painful to express a feeling or need and not have the person to whom you made the expression validate or fulfill it. And so, the coping strategy for Enneagram 2s in the face of expressed but unvalidated feelings is to suppress their own feelings and needs.

The problem, however, is that Enneagram 2s are deep feelers. Feeling is their primary center of intelligence, relied upon more than doing or thinking. So, if they stop feeling their own feelings, they are still going to respond to feelings—just not their own any longer.

Enneagram 2s quickly learn that sensing, anticipating, and meeting the feelings and needs of other people earn them a special place. If they can meet and respond to the feelings and needs of people around them, even before others express their needs, Enneagram 2s discover that other people come to rely on them or, in some cases, even need them. Overserving validates their position in relationships and gives them a sense of security that other people will not abandon them because they have become indispensable.

It is not difficult to see how the pattern of pushing down one's own feelings and needs and anticipating the feelings and needs of other people can lead to codependent or enabling relationships, where one person adopts the role of the "giver," and the other person adopts the role of the "taker." When Enneagram 2s honestly inventory their lives, they will always find evidence of codependent behavior in at least one season.

Pride in Enneagram 2s is not about accomplishments or successes, it's about place. They take pride in their place as the helper, the rescuer, the fixer, and the giver in relationship to loved ones. Enneagram 2s come to relationships saying, "The good news is that I'm doing fine. I don't need anything, which means that I can devote all my energy to anticipating and addressing your feelings and needs." Their script usually works as a successful strategy to earn belonging in relationships for a while, but it almost always results in pain. Sometimes the pain comes from the other person feeling coddled or smothered and telling the Enneagram 2 to leave them alone. Other times, the other person is glad for the overattention, but eventually the Enneagram 2 burns out from helping and is finally confronted with their own need, only to realize that they have curated a one-sided relationship and the other person is less interested in meeting their needs.

Pride is born from pain. Enneagram 2s adopt a painful belief that because the people you love most can't or won't validate your feelings and needs in the way that you want them validated, you must push them down. Enneagram 2s are protecting themselves through their self-deferential and self-defacing strategies.

If I never share how I feel, then people cannot fail to validate my feelings. If I never share what I need, then I protect myself from people whom I love letting me down. The longer that pride is the motivating force behind their actions, the more out of touch Enneagram 2s become with their own feelings and needs, so that when they encounter other people who are genuinely interested in them, they have lost the ability to respond to genuine invitations for self-revelation.

The motivating pride of an Enneagram 2 becomes so instinctual that when faced with a question or invitation from someone toward self-disclosure, they can only defer, avoid, and pivot. It's true that this number is the giver and the helper of the Enneagram, but imagine if all that giving and helping came from a motivating impulse of humility rather than pride. Imagine if they could disclose their own feelings and needs, allowing other people to surprise them by meeting them. Can you imagine the beautiful mutuality that would become possible in relationships if Enneagram 2s, operating from a place of humility rather than pride, could find that other people want to know, validate, and have the chance to meet their feelings and needs? What a gift!

At their core, Enneagram 2s want deep love, connection, and belonging. Relationships are everything to them. But when they approach relationships from a place of pride, they sabotage the potential for true mutuality as they bake position and power into the relationship. To find the love and belonging they so desperately want, they must find their way, through recovery of their virtue of humility, to vulnerable and authentic self-disclosure. It is in sharing our true stories that we find lasting places to belong.

Enneagram 3s: From Truthfulness to Deceit

The core passion for Enneagram 3s is deceit. Their primary deceit is self-deceit rather than an intention to deceive others. Their story begins with the virtue of truthfulness. And in our Enneagram context, truthfulness refers to the ability to discern and faithfully bear out inner truths. In a performance- and success-driven culture, it's important to understand that career is not the only aspect of the Enneagram 3's life where the virtue of truthfulness is born out. Many Enneagram 3s do have successful careers, but truthfulness goes deeper than just picking out the job that is most right for you.

Somewhere along the way, the world steps in and Enneagram 3s discover that their environment is not as interested and/or accepting of their truest ways of being and that love is easier to earn when they remake themselves into the image of their community. And they have a special ability to become something they are not. Out of all the feelers on the Enneagram, which are 2s, 3s, and 4s—those who give priority to feeling as the center of intelligence most relied upon—Enneagram 3s are the best at shapeshifting to accommodate their context. When you are especially sensitive to feelings, both your own and those of others, you can manipulate (in the broadest meaning of the word) the way you relate to your context because you can intuit how people will receive and accept you based on how you choose to act.

And so, young Enneagram 3s show up first as themselves, but in the face of indifference or nonacceptance, they rely on their powers of discernment to discover a more acceptable way to show up in their context. As they adopt a contextualized self and receive the affirmations that come along with it, they lean further into the adaptation they are projecting and, after a while, they have mastered their new way of showing up in the world.

Once their pattern of discerning and adapting to context happens often enough, and if the rewards are great enough, adapting to environmental cues becomes so natural to Enneagram 3s that they forget they are doing it, and the passion of deceit really takes root. By the time they are teenagers or young adults, they will no longer recognize the ways their adaptations are inconsistent with their deeper understanding of true self.

It usually takes a big failure for an Enneagram 3 to stop their constant habit of adapting to context and wake up to a truer awareness of who they really are at their core—reawakening their precious virtue of truthfulness. *But who wants to fail, right?!* And they are more likely to succeed than fail, absent uncontrollable outside interventions, so soul work, or virtue-reclaiming, is harder for them than for most of the other Enneagram types. Enneagram 3s have some of the most adaptive strategies, which usually means that their personality seems to work for them longer than it does for many of the rest of us.

Truthfulness, for Enneagram 3s, is about a deep commitment to take an inward journey far enough and long enough to discern who they truly are. Through the virtue of truthfulness, they will have all the gifts and graces necessary to discern and commit to being truly themselves in every aspect of their lives. The contributions that last beyond a person's lifetime and become the things of legacy are born only from humans who are bearing out their own gifts, not the copies of gifts that they think are most prized. Only the real you is memorable.

Enneagram 4s: From Equanimity to Envy

The passion for Enneagram 4s is envy. From the start, we need to remember the difference between envy and jealousy. Jealousy usually has a more particular focus than envy. We can become jealous of another person's car, money, career, partner, or looks. Envy goes deeper. It usually involves looking at someone else's life and imagining that their whole way of being is better or more desirable than your own and wishing that you could have what they have. It begins with admiration of another person but quickly turns from the positive emotion of admiration to something more poisonous when you are no longer content to admire from afar but instead are compelled to become the focus of your admiration.

For Enneagram 4s, the most common iteration of envy is the desire to have what they perceive as an ease of living that another person has. In their own minds, life is hard on Enneagram 4s. For as long as they can remember, they have felt misunderstood and outside of the group. Their strong connection to and experience with the full emotional spectrum—especially the outer poles of that spectrum and not the balanced center—has set them up to feel like everyone always wants them to be a little less "extra" or a little more "toned down." Their self-perception is that other Enneagram types have an easier and more "normal" experience of life because of their more regulated emotions.

But the challenge goes deeper as Enneagram 4s live in the push-pull of envying others' normalness while also relishing their otherness and truly feeling that the worst thing to be would be normal. *How bland and uninteresting life would be to be normal*, they think. They play out a game of emotional-relational push-pull through their passion of envy. In every object of envy for the Enneagram 4, something is admired and hoped for, and something is resented and scoffed at. They live in the complicated tangling of the both-and.

Somewhere along the way, Enneagram 4s hide away their virtue of equanimity and its emotional regulation and balance, protecting themselves from perceptions of the world's lack of acceptance. Envy becomes the chief guard and defense for the precious, true core of equanimity, which leads to the exact opposite emotional outflow of equanimity—replacing temperance and balance with emotional swings and instability.

Enneagram 4s learn to live in the energy-boosting chaos of a dynamic and dramatic emotional experience. Balanced and tempered emotions no longer hold appeal. Only the farthest poles of both sides of the emotional spectrum seem interesting and alive. Their virtue of equanimity, hidden further away, becomes harder to connect to as the passion of envy settles in.

I met Valerie at an Enneagram coaching session where she asked for an hour of my time to work through some experiences that she wanted to reconcile as an Enneagram 4. As we started our session together, I asked her in as open-ended a way as possible to tell me about her nature in her own words. Her story still captivates me and is one of the clearest articulations of the push-pull experienced by the Enneagram 4.

Valerie told me that when she was in her early twenties, she attended college in California. One of her favorite practices during that season of her life was to go to the beach early in the morning to watch the sunrise. She would take her fold-up camp chair, a thick blanket, and her Walkman (*Hey, millennials!*) to play, in her words, her "moody music soundtrack." As she sat in her chair, music on, watching the sun rise over the Pacific Ocean, she would dream and visualize the things that she hoped to have in the future: a spouse, kids, a satisfying career. She said that she had a dream of buying a big fixer-upper house with her husband early in their marriage so they could raise their children there and never move, that their grandchildren would one day visit the same house where their parents had grown up. Valerie told me that during the long and sometimes lonely days of college, those solitary mornings on the beach, and the visualizations that she fantasized about, gave her energy and longing that felt so good.

Fast-forward twenty years to the day when Valerie was sitting on my couch, telling me her story. She told me that she had gotten married and that she and her husband had three well-loved kids. They had bought the house that she dreamed of and that, if all went according to script, her children would be able to bring their children to the same home one day. Her whole beachside dream had come to fruition. But she was still unhappy in some ways. Her lingering unhappiness had prompted her to look for tools like the

Enneagram and the inner work that it spurs. Valerie told me that the only thing she wanted now was to be able to go back to that beach, early in the morning, in her twenties, and one more time, "taste the longing of what it felt like to dream for all of the things that she now had before she had them." What felt missing from her life was the longing, the waiting, and the anticipation.

Valerie's story illustrates the beautiful, complex nuance of the passion of envy in Enneagram 4s. Many are trapped in the constant pushes and pulls that envy creates, where the fantasy is greater than their experience of the actual thing. Getting the things in life that they worked toward or hoped for also comes with disappointment and a sense of loss. And the loss is for the longing, the waiting, the anticipating.

Only through resurrection of the virtue of equanimity and the tempered emotions, satisfaction, and completeness that it can bring can Enneagram 4s let go of the fantasy long enough to experience the joy of the real thing. Through a commitment to inner work and a therapeutic journey, Valerie has begun to savor the extraordinary gift of home, family, pet, and career. She began practicing presence-oriented spiritual practices, like centering prayer, to train herself to detach from thoughts and fantasies, grounding herself in holy awareness of the now. Enneagram 4s must learn to let go of their idealization of the past and fantasied future so that they can fully mine the moment that they are in, no matter how regular, ordinary, or dull, to reveal all the moment's holy ordinariness.

Enneagram 5s: From Nonattachment to Greed

In Enneagram 5s, the virtue of nonattachment translates into the passion of greed. The specific forms greed takes is specific to each person of this type. They may feel greed for money or specific items, but for every Enneagram 5, greed is principally about their commitment to accumulate and guard their own personal store of time, energy, affection, and privacy.

Enneagram 5s zealously guard their time, which feels limited to them and uniquely their own. If you want some of their time, you can petition them for it, and they will decide on their own terms whether to give it to you.

The journey from virtue to passion for Enneagram 5s takes them from a place of contented openhandedness described through the virtue of nonattachment, where they know they have enough of everything and will not run out, to the development of the passion of greed born from a gnawing fear that maybe there isn't more where that came from—so they learn to ration and hoard their limited resources. Somewhere along the Enneagram 5's journey, the lie of scarcity takes root. Their experience of the world teaches them that resources may run dry, causing them to forget over time all about their innate virtue of contented nonattachment.

For Enneagram 5s, energy can feel like manna. They must thoughtfully ration and measure out each fresh daily serving so they can reach the end of the day before they run out. Similarly, affection comes with a beginning and an end, and they must dole it out thoughtfully. Physical touch, hugs, and intimacy all take something out of the Enneagram 5. Even when affection is what they want to give, they are aware of the cost and energy output. Finally, privacy is especially important to Enneagram 5s. A sense of limited reserves for time and energy causes them to zealously guard their privacy and independence.

Enneagram 5s are an interior-oriented number more than they are an exterior-oriented number. It is rare, though not impossible, to discover one who describes themselves as an extrovert. They relish time alone and feel that solitude centers them, recharges them, and gives them time to explore the personal interests that really matter to them the most. Infringements of their privacy can feel like anger-producing violations to Enneagram 5s, who would never think about invading someone else's privacy or personal space.

While the passion of greed leads Enneagram 5s to continually inventory and measure out their storehouses of time, energy, affection, and privacy, the resource that they pursue and hoard the most is the most commonly available resource of all: information and knowledge. Enneagram 5s are experts in one or more subjects, not necessarily connected to their work or income-generating activities. They all feel comforted by knowing a little bit more about a lot of things than others know.

I met a woman named Jean at an Enneagram event that I led in upstate New York. Jean was a beloved and much-relied-upon member of her community. But despite her seeming belovedness and deep connections within her church and neighborhood, she told me during a lunch break that she "gets people poisoning." We laughed together as she explained that despite her love for her friends and her place in her community, sometimes enough is enough and she has to escape! Caught navigating the complex balance between wanting both connection and solitude, most Enneagram 5s can sympathize with Jean's feelings. Whenever I teach Enneagram workshops for couples, I tell those who have a partner that is an Enneagram 5 that it is braver for this number to show up in relationship than it is for all the other types because the perceived cost is so much greater.

The lifetime of spiritual work offered to 5s through the wisdom of the Enneagram and contemplation is to move steadily toward the adoption of an abundance mindset rather than a scarcity mindset. Moving from a scarcity mindset to an abundance mindset requires risk. The only way that an Enneagram 5 can rewire their mindset is through confrontation with the risk of running out. They will not intuitively feel that there is more where that came from or that the world will put into their hands what they need; so, Enneagram 5s have to practice mini opportunities where they face the risk of running out. I don't encourage Enneagram 5s to give away their whole retirement account as a way of rewiring from scarcity to abundance, but maybe they can indulge themselves in one purchase this month that feels extravagant. Maybe they can say "yes" to one more social outing this week than they would normally allow themselves to accept. These small-stakes opportunities to experiment with the terrifying (which it truly is to an Enneagram 5) potential of running out are safe ways to begin the virtuous journey. Rewriting the script in their minds from lack to plenty will help Enneagram 5s find their way back to recovering the precious virtue of nonattachment hidden within.

Enneagram 6s: From Courage to Fear

The passion for Enneagram 6s is fear. And just as I reframed their traditionally named virtue of courage to faith, a more helpful word for their passion is *anxiety* rather than *fear*. Enneagram 6s are neither crippled nor defeated by their fear. Their fear, which really takes the form of an ever-present, latent anxiety, gives them energy and motivation. Anxiety does not paralyze them; it helps them to be prepared. They feel that their anxiety—experienced like an elevator's ever-present mood music—helps them know what they need to plan for.

Remember that the personalities of our Enneagram numbers point to our deepest motivations, not principally the ways in which we behave. And while several Enneagram types wrestle with a looming anxiety that feels constant, the source and focus of the anxiety is distinct to each individual Enneagram type. Enneagram 1s have anxiety that they will not be able to get it—whatever *it* is—right. Enneagram 2s have lots of anxious thoughts about relationships ending and what they have potentially done to cause it. Enneagram 4s have anxiety about not fitting in. Enneagram 5s are anxious that they might run out of something they need.

And Enneagram 7s feel a great amount of anxiety anytime they are trapped in pain or grief—their own or someone else's—without an easy path of escape.

The anxiety, or fear, that Enneagram 6s experience is more externalized. They worry about all the things that could go wrong that are outside of their control. They feel comforted by making plans and further contingencies in case their plans do not work. When Enneagram 6s have plans that make sense to them, they can relax, at least regarding one specific focus of anxiety, and give their brain space to something else.

My friend Jill, an Enneagram 6, likes to take Saturday morning walks with her daughter Adie at a nature reserve close to their house in Nashville. Adie, an Enneagram 4, is a budding photographer and takes her camera on the hikes with her mother, capturing the beauty of Radnor Lake and its surroundings. Many times, when Jill and Adie return home, they will look at the photographs that Adie captured. Jill told me that when they scroll through the images, she feels like she must not have been on the same hike. Where was she when Adie captured the family of grazing deer through the leaves? she wonders. Where was she when Adie saw the beautiful orange mushroom growing out of the face of the rock? She realized that she never sees any of the same things that Adie sees, even though they walked the same trail side by side. After months of reflecting on her consistent reaction, she finally figured out the mystery. "I was looking for snakes!" she exclaimed. While Adie had her head up, observing the sights and sounds around them, Jill had her head down, surveying the two or three feet in front of them for snakes.

The potential for danger *is* everywhere. Enneagram 6s get that part right. The problem for them is that the possibility of danger looms so large in their minds, through the evolution and growth of their passion of anxiety or fear, that they come to not only anticipate danger but also to expect it. And the expectation of danger—in all the forms that danger takes—keeps their focus off the good, *the wonderful*, the beautiful surprises happening all around them.

As with every other Enneagram type, everything begins in virtue for Enneagram 6s. Courage and faith come at the beginning of their story. But somewhere along the way, they feel caught off guard one too many times and their sense of the benevolence and stability of the world is lost. They regain a sense of control and power over the seeming randomness and overwhelming dangers of the world by placing themselves on the watchtower. They stand vigilant and ready for whatever may come, no matter the likelihood that the anticipated danger will happen or not.

The spiritual invitation for Enneagram 6s is to relearn Frederick Buechner's advice: "Here is the world; beautiful and terrible things will happen; be not afraid."[1] Only through tethering themselves to a story that is greater than their own—a spiritual story that connects all things and all peoples in a way that makes all things well—can Enneagram 6s rediscover the faith, their precious gift, hidden inside.

Enneagram 7s: From Sobriety to Gluttony

The passion for Enneagram 7s is gluttony. They have an insatiable appetite for experiences, a drive to squeeze as much out of life as possible. Their near compulsion for new adventures and new experiences can take many forms. Some are travel enthusiasts, others are foodies, and still others are serial entrepreneurs. The main focuses of their gluttony are personal to the Enneagram 7.

Some Enneagram 7s who are foodies tell me that when they go to a new restaurant, they find the menu online in advance and enjoy the thrill of reading the full set of options. They dream about the possibility of ordering the entire menu and sampling each item. These same Enneagram 7s tell me that when their meal arrives, the actual experience of eating the item they chose was often not as pleasurable as they imagined the experience would be.

The difficulty that Enneagram 7s face as the passion of gluttony takes root is to find satisfaction in anything. Just as someone who is drug or alcohol dependent needs more of the substance over time to get the same high as at the beginning, Enneagram 7s can fall into a pattern of pursuing more and more. For them, gluttony is the easiest, most readily accessible, and preferred entry point into the room of passions, but once their feature passion of gluttony is embraced, they find themselves in a room of passions that includes all nine—anger, pride, deceit, envy, greed, fear, gluttony, lust, and sloth.

Like the rest of us, Enneagram 7s carry a wound—albeit a well-hidden one. For this number, the wounding message adopted in childhood is wisely captured by the pioneering Enneagram work of Don Richard Riso and Russ Hudson: you better not depend on anybody for anything.[2] You should be self-reliant and make your own way through the world. Make your own path, your own fun, and your own adventure. Because at the end of the day, you will end up alone. Behind the mask of fun making, adventure seeking, and load lightening is a message from early childhood that haunts Enneagram 7s and drives them toward self-reliance. Carrying the message that you should not depend on anybody for anything is a burden that contributes to their suffering. When you believe that the people around you may not be present to you consistently, loneliness settles over you. The loneliness and the suffering that follows give birth to the passion of gluttony for Enneagram 7s.

In the journey from true self to false self for Enneagram 7s, life begins with the virtue of sobriety. The capacity for sobriety, sober judgment, and moderation is one of the truest things that you could say about this number. True sobriety in practice for Enneagram 7s looks like accepting negative emotions, being content in less, voluntarily giving up control over your enjoyment and circumstances, and savoring small things over and over again instead of continually being on the hunt for new and more. When young people of this type experience suffering, their wound takes the shape of the opposite of what's truest about them: their passion. So, Enneagram 7s project gluttony when truly they have the deepest capacity for sobriety of all the personalities on the Enneagram. It is one of life's great mysteries that what is truest about us often feels the scariest to reveal.

Because sobriety embodies their true self, the journey from gluttony to sobriety is a return—a journey home to what is fundamentally true. Enneagram 7s do not need to grab hold of sobriety; they need to let go of gluttony. Sobriety was always there; sobriety will always be there. The question is whether they can remove the mask of gluttony to reveal what has always lived underneath: sobriety.

Enneagram 8s: From Innocence to Lust

The passion for Enneagram 8s is lust. In our traditional connotations for lust, we think of intimacy, intensity, and passion. And these are certainly appropriate words for describing Enneagram 8s, who will often express to me that if their experience with a partner—romantic or otherwise—was not intense, the event didn't feel important. Enneagram 8s move toward people and experiences that carry a charge promising the same excitement and intensity of a sexual charge. They are passionate people. When we describe them as feeling-repressed, which just means that they rely on doing and thinking as their primary centers of intelligence rather than feeling, they will often push back. "I feel deeply and strongly," Enneagram 8s tell me. And in some respects, they are right, but the question is: Have they mistaken their passion for feeling? Sure, they are passionate people. Far from having a flat affect, they are charged up and can be spark plugs in relationships. But passion is not the same thing as deep feeling. To feel deeply means to open yourself to the full spectrum of emotions and to see the ways in which the highs and lows of the emotional spectrum are inextricably linked together. You can experience the greatest emotional highs of extraordinary joy and elation only when you are also well acquainted and comfortable with the deepest lows of sorrow and despair.

Enneagram 8s are not particularly adept or comfortable in the lower regions of the emotional spectrum. Their passion of lust limits their interest and engagement with softer, tenderer feelings. *Gentle*, *meek*, and *lowly* sound like the words of a Christmas carol to them, never as something that they would aspire to be.

Lust stunts Enneagram 8s because their constant need for turned-up emotional experiences means they overlook the tender beauty of ordinary moments. Vulnerability, softness, tenderness, and quiet are not privileged by Enneagram 8s, so they miss a lot of living. They can be physically or psychologically absent when the rest of us are processing grief or savoring a quiet moment.

Betrayal, or the perception of it, comes early for this number. Because innocence is their virtue, Enneagram 8s have an intrinsic openness and vulnerability to offer to the world, but somewhere their vulnerability is met by perceived betrayal. They hide the soft, tender, and "innocent" parts of themselves so that the betrayals and dangers of the world cannot penetrate. They build boundaries. Trust is withdrawn and replaced with skepticism. Enneagram 8s do not wither or fade when they learn how the world truly works. They are said to have more energy than all the other Enneagram types. And because of their high energy and great natural abilities, instead of wilting in fear, 8s bloom as the passion of lust grows. They become intense, passionate, tough, and slightly (or not so slightly!) intimidating to the rest of us.

At an Enneagram event that I taught at a church, the associate pastor—Rob, an Enneagram 8—described himself by saying: "I have a big heart; it's just wrapped up in razor wire." *I'm not sure that I have heard a better description for the Enneagram 8!* Their hearts are big. Their feelings are big. They care a lot. They love hard. They have hearts for the underdog and the energy to confront the oppressor. They are justice makers. They are movement builders. But their early experiences with and perceptions of betrayal by those they loved the most caused them to build fences of razor wire around their hearts so that they could protect themselves from future hurt.

The problem is that these defenses are not only protecting Enneagram 8s from pain but are also keeping them from experiencing the full depths of love and connection that they want most deeply. Their goal in life cannot be to protect themselves from every betrayal, because if protection from betrayal is the goal, their defenses will be so high and so well built that in addition to protecting themselves from pain, they will protect themselves from love.

The deepest experiences of openhearted, swing-wide-the-gates love always come with a chance that someone will hurt us along the way. Lovers sometimes leave. Marriages and friendships end. Passion can dim. But the payoff for opening ourselves to the possibility of pain are the moments and years—however few—of great love. And great love does not live in a walled-off garden. Great love grows like a vine that escapes every boundary to grow where it grows and travel where it travels.

The recovery of the virtue of innocence allows Enneagram 8s to open themselves to deeper feelings than they ever knew were possible. They can recapture the innocent and infectious joy of a child or a puppy in even greater measure than the other Enneagram types can experience. Innocence is their virtue, their precious gift, their pearl of great price. As Enneagram 8s shed the layers of lust, built by their passion, they will discover innocence and the gifts that innocence brings to a life previously characterized by competition, control, and cynicism.

Enneagram 9s: From Action to Sloth

The passion for Enneagram 9s is sloth. While connotations for sloth evoke laziness, this type is not lazy in the traditional sense. We think of lazy people as people who do not do very much or who are the opposite of busy. But Enneagram 9s are often just as busy or busier than the rest of us. My friend Carmen, an Enneagram 9, sent me a meme[3] a few months ago that she said perfectly described her day:

> I needed to do the laundry, but then I realized I was out of detergent, so I went to write a shopping list

> and realized how unorganized the junk drawer was and started checking pens for ink. When I went to toss all the junk, I saw that the trash was full but before I took it out, I wanted to get rid of old food in the fridge. That's when I realized a juice jug had leaked so I needed to clean it up but when I went to grab a rag, I saw that the pantry closet was a nightmare, so I started organizing it. And that's how I ended up on the floor looking at my old photo albums from the 1990s and not doing laundry.

Many Enneagram 9s will resonate with how Carmen connected this description to the ways her days veer off course. Sloth for this type takes two main forms. First, sloth can manifest as busyness that distracts or procrastinates from the things that the Enneagram 9 really meant to do. In the meme, the plan was to do laundry, but the laundry never got done because there were so many other things that the Enneagram 9 chose to do first. Those lesser activities gave them permission to not get to the laundry because they were busy with other things. The Enneagram 9 here was not being "lazy"; they were terribly busy!

Sloth for Enneagram 9s can be a way of giving themselves permission to not get to the things that they know they really need to do, but that may be hard or that they just simply do not want to do, because they are so busy doing other things. Procrastination feels acceptable and even excusable for 9s because, after all, they were doing *something*! It's not like they were on the couch being lazy—though every Enneagram 9 does appreciate lazy time on the couch—so they can give themselves a break for not doing the hard things.

The things that Enneagram 9s procrastinate are things they aren't sure they know how to do, things that might cause conflict with someone else, things that might threaten their inner sense of balance and peace, or things that would require them to assert themselves.

The second way sloth can show up for Enneagram 9s is as a desire to be unaffected by life. People of this type do not want anything to disturb their inner quiet. They want to get through life as unscathed and unbruised as possible. They would rather go unnoticed than make a big splash that leads to controversy. If they can get through life without upsetting others and without others upsetting them, that would feel like success. Yet the existential question remains for Enneagram 9s: Did you get to the things that you really meant to do? Have you accomplished anything hard? Or do you have regrets because you always thought there would be more time, but somehow the time slipped away while you were busy with lesser things?

I encourage Enneagram 9s to periodically incorporate some sort of regrets analysis into their lives so that they can inventory the things that they meant to get to and challenge themselves to get to those things before energy or time runs out. Putting off hard things by keeping busy with lesser things and the desire to be unaffected by life are the slothful ways in which Enneagram 9s stay trapped in their passion.

Remember that the absence of conflict does not mean the presence of peace. Sometimes brokering a lasting peace, internally and externally, requires conflict, or at least the possibility for conflict. The passion of sloth does not solve the deeper inner and outer conflicts that Enneagram 9s know are bubbling beneath the surface. But sloth and the numbing procrastination that sloth brings help 9s temporarily forget about the hard things, the scary things, the exciting things, and the risky things that they know they must get to in their lifetimes.

Only through finding and rekindling the underlying virtue of action—better described as *right action*—can Enneagram 9s escape a lifetime of regrets and the deep tiredness that habitual numbing strategies bring.

With knowledge comes power—the power to change and the power to allow yourself to be open to God's process of transformation. Through relinking the passions and the virtues, as one unified Enneagram discipline, we have revealed the fundamental Enneagram mystery hiding in plain sight: we begin in virtue, but our passion forms early in life as a mechanism to protect our virtue. And as our passion builds, we forget that there was ever a virtue hiding underneath. Through the transformative work of contemplation, which we will turn to next, we can let go of passion and uncover virtue.

5

Contemplative Spirituality as a Way of Life

At dinner one evening, my friends Joe and Suzanne Stabile told me that they were making plans to launch a second year-long cohort program at their ministry center in Dallas. For years, Suzanne had been leading a variety of immersive programs at the Micah Center for people to facilitate intensive growth around the Enneagram. Due to the popularity of these programs, Joe and Suzanne realized there was a growing hunger for deep work in small communities that met for an entire year. And with Joe nearing a mandatory retirement age in his denominational church, he had begun to think about launching a year-long cohort of his own.

Over dinner, Joe told me that the cohort would explore the intersection between contemplation and Enneagram wisdom and that he had already talked to a pastor in Nashville—a dear friend of mine—about leading the cohort with him. Joe asked me to come for the first weekend of the year-long cohort to teach a Know Your Number workshop so that all participants could begin the year in a common place of Enneagram language.

Several months after our first conversation, Joe called to let me know that my friend in Nashville who was originally scheduled to colead the cohort with him had to withdraw for scheduling reasons. Joe asked me if I would like to fill in as the cohort's coleader. I jumped at the chance, welcoming the opportunity to learn about a topic that reached inside of me and pulled me close, but one that I did not know much about: contemplative spirituality.

Our first year of the Contemplative Cohort was thrilling for me. As Joe and I planned our quarterly gatherings, I created a schedule for us that consisted of an alternating series of sessions—an Enneagram session, followed by a contemplative teaching by Joe, back to an Enneagram session, and so on. When each of my Enneagram teaching sessions ended, I eagerly took my seat in the back of the room and tried to write down every word that Joe was saying.

Some of the practices that Joe taught were familiar—at least in name—to practices that I had learned about in my evangelical experience, like fasting, Sabbath keeping, and almsgiving. Other practices, like liturgy of the hours and centering prayer, were brand new to me. These practices that were more about being than thinking—undergoing rather than undertaking—were the balm that my starved soul needed. I wanted to be a contemplative. And even though my understanding of what it meant to be a contemplative was limited, I knew contemplation was a posture I wanted to adopt.

What Does Contemplation Mean?

To understand the origins of contemplation, consider the earliest centuries of Christian Church history. After several hundred years of Christianity (or the Way of Jesus, as it was originally known) steadily growing as a minority tradition of belief across the Roman Empire, the Roman emperor embraced Christianity. With an evangelist as head of state, Christianity evolved from a developing, minor religion to a mainstream, state-sponsored tradition. Some followers of the Way embraced their newfound cultural status and were glad to see their convictions spreading throughout the region. They celebrated seeing new churches built, new bishops consecrated, and new power and influence for followers of the Christian tradition.

But other followers of the Way of Jesus became disillusioned at what seemed like new excesses and opportunities for corruption in a church that had become embedded in the world of politics, power, and money. Some of these followers of the Way left the modern Roman cities behind and moved out into more remote locations, specifically desert frontiers in Egypt, Palestine, Arabia, and beyond. Today, we refer to these spiritual ancestors as the desert mothers and fathers.

The origins of the monastic movement are found in the witness of the desert mothers and fathers who left Rome for a simpler life in austere locations that would allow them to renounce the excesses of a state-sponsored religious program and rediscover the Way of Jesus, specifically in commitment to simplicity, poverty, and spiritual purity.

From the third to the sixth century, the movement of Christian communities flourishing outside of the institutional church grew and became known as contemplative spirituality. Borrowing from the traditions and practices that had emerged from the institutional Christian Church, these desert mothers and fathers also created new stripped-down practices as a way of experiencing a Christian spirituality that was more about inner growth, soul work, and simplicity of living. Their path stood in contrast to the growing influence of the Church of Rome and its increasing alignment with the state.

These seekers living on the edges and frontiers of known Roman society seemed strange to most people of the time, in the same way that monks, nuns, and cloistered religious people seem strange to many of us today. The desert mothers and fathers renounced materialism, looked at those in power with suspicion, and found joy in a simple way of living while focusing on the inner life of the soul rather than on the outer life of accomplishments.

These spiritual pioneers sought to live a life closer to that observed by Jesus of Nazareth and his earliest followers. Foundations of prayer, silence, and intentional economy of living—only having what you need and shunning the world's ways of accumulating, counting, and hoarding—undergirded the loose movement that was the precursor to the monastic movement. They created many of the communities and rules for living that are still practiced today, such as the *Rule of St. Benedict.* From the pathway of these spiritual pioneers, we find the seeds of contemplation.

Modern contemplative teacher James Finley wrote that "a contemplative discipline [or practice] is any act habitually entered into with your whole heart as a way of awakening, deepening, and sustaining a contemplative experience of the inherent holiness of the present moment."[1] Writer and former monk Thomas Moore, in his *Meditations: On the Monk Who Dwells in Daily Life*, describes contemplation as "cutting out a space for [the divine]."[2]

Contemplative living is built from a foundation of several tenets, each evidenced in the life of Jesus and regained and fleshed out by the desert mothers and fathers. These tenets include

belief that God is everywhere in everything;
commitment to the present moment;
acknowledgment that the work is God's, not ours; and
practice of simplicity in living.

As we envision these foundational principles as the guideposts for a new way of living, we will become contemplatives. Being a contemplative is less about what you do and more about how you see. It's about intention and attention more than any action you can take.

On the first day that you commit yourself to the belief that God is everywhere in everything, that you must become attuned to the present moment, that the work is God's and not ours, and that simplicity in living is the pathway to peace, you have joined the contemplative journey. *You are a contemplative. As simple as that.*

Everyone can take the contemplative journey, not just the monks, nuns, and priests among us. Every action can become a contemplative action. Every practice, a contemplative practice.

After describing how contemplative practices are less about the "what" and more about the "why," I hesitate to suggest a list of practices for fear that I am contributing to the incorrect belief that there is some right way to enter contemplation. But if you promise to keep this belief at bay and continue to hear me suggest that any act can become a contemplative act and that contemplation is a posture for living rather than a scorecard to grade, I will share some practices that have been personally meaningful to me in my emerging contemplative journey.

Like many people endeavoring toward contemplation, centering prayer has become a particularly meaningful practice to me. I'll list it first here in my summary of practices to underscore the way in which I believe that it animates and provides foundation for most of the other practices. Many contemplative teachers instruct students to practice centering prayer habitually, while the other practices may weave in and out of the seasons of your life.

As I am writing this book, these are some of the practices that have been especially meaningful to me. If you are new to the contemplative journey and want a practice or two to try on, you might draw from this list. If you have already been exploring and experimenting with contemplative practices for a while, keep exploring the ones that have become meaningful to you.

Centering Prayer

The Intention: To be totally open to the presence and activity of God.

The Why: By stilling our bodies and quieting our thoughts, we give up our role of agency over our spiritual lives and submit ourselves to God's internal rearranging that is unseen and unobservable by us.

The What: Sit in silence for up to twenty minutes, but it's okay to begin with five. Sit in a chair in a quiet space, with your legs and arms uncrossed. Close your eyes and focus on your breathing. Practice letting go of your thoughts. Each time a thought enters your mind (and hundreds or thousands will), return your attention to your breath or, if the thoughts are still too hard to detach from, focus your intention on one sacred word (maybe *beloved*) as a way of returning to the practice and returning to your intention. Don't cling to any thought—even if the thought shows up as epiphany or revelation of some question that you have been holding. Trust that if a thought is sent from God, it will return to your mind during your ordinary awareness at some point after your centering prayer is over. After the bell or timer rings, letting you know that your five or twenty minutes have passed, get up and return to your day. The only way to get centering prayer "wrong" is to not do it or to get up during the middle of it and quit.

Silence

The Intention: To be totally open to the presence and activity of God.

The Why: Our world is crowded with rushing and noise, and in silence we find our way back to God's first language. In the Hebrew Bible's description of creation, all begins in silence and then God speaks. Returning to silence returns us to God's original state of rest before God's activity began, and returning to silence makes room in our hearts and lives for God to speak and begin God's work of creating something new in us.

The What: Find your way to silence for a period of time. Turning off the radio on your car ride home can be a practice of silence. Sitting on your porch swing for an hour can be a practice of silence. Silence is a different practice from centering prayer, so you don't have to be as rigid or committed to unfocused attention or escaping of thoughts. Just let the moment be the moment. You can follow your mind where it leads you, but let the sound of nature or the quiet hum of electricity through the house be your companion rather than speech, music, television, or any other noise that we so often choose for our company.

Pilgrimage

The Intention: To be totally open to the presence and activity of God.

The Why: Sacred texts are filled with stories of journey. We learn new things on journeys, and we remember old things on journeys. Pilgrimage is primarily about the remembrance of something old rather than the taking on of something new. Pilgrims have traveled to Mecca, Jerusalem, Lourdes, and other places all over the world as a way of remembering and discovering something significant that happened in those places—whether something of history or lore. This kind of travel is a way of placing yourself amid a story that is older than yourself. When I traveled to Bethlehem and placed my hand on a rock in the basement of an old church built on top of the stable where, supposedly, the baby Jesus was born, I was remembering the birth of Jesus in a physical way in a place where millions of people have centered their collective attention on his story.

The What: Pilgrimage can happen anywhere. You can take a pilgrimage on the Camino or to Bethlehem, like

I did. But you can also take a pilgrimage to your childhood home or to the church where your grandmother was baptized. In these places, you remember something about who you are, who you were, and where you come from. Pilgrimage can be made to places of warm memory and to places of great pain. The act of remembering is conflicted with the good and the bad. Pilgrimage stirs up both. The journey of a pilgrim involves a hope that when you return home, something from the journey will have changed you. It may be the spot you meant to travel to, or it may be the people you meet along the way, but pilgrimage is a physical means to remember your history, your people, and your stories.

Sabbath Keeping

The Intention: To be totally open to the presence and activity of God.

The Why: Beyond the "God told us to do it" matter of obligation from Genesis's list of dos and don'ts, Sabbath keeping is an important component in a balanced life. Our culture is driven to produce, work, and achieve. Sabbath keeping is a way of taking ourselves off the throne of control and world agency and relearning in our rest that God's work continues even when we do not. And this is an important thing to remember! As long as we are the doers and the makers, we can forget that we are not gods.

The What: Take a day—traditionally observed from sundown to sundown—to pray and play, as characterized by Eugene H. Peterson in his book *Working the Angles.*[3] Traditional Sabbath begins at sundown because it begins in rest. You sleep first, because sleep is the deepest embodiment of rest. In the words of Peterson, you pray and you play when you wake up the next day. As simple as that. I won't give any further explanation for the praying and playing because we are so hungry—me included—for lists and steps. Just pray and play, and don't work! That's it. Sabbath rest, *oh, how we need it.*

Puzzle Working

The Intention: To be totally open to the presence and activity of God.

The Why: Taking something that was whole but then broken apart and putting it back together again slows us down, focuses our attention away from our dreaming and scheming, and practices God's work of taking broken things and putting them back to right.

The What: Spend a minute centering on the intention and then do a puzzle! As simple as that. All you're doing through your puzzle working is reminding yourself that God's work is a work of re-creating and re-membering broken things. Nothing that is torn apart can ever be lost to God. God, in God's time, makes all things whole whether we can see it or not. And how incredible that God invites us—like in our puzzle making—to join God's work!

Wisdom Friends

The Intention: To be totally open to the presence and activity of God.

The Why: Mentorship and intergenerational friendship are tested and true ways to expand your mind and heart. Who has not benefited from deep friendship with someone who is clearly a wisdom person?

The What: Think of wisdom people who live in your community. You know the ones—*no definition for wisdom person needed.* Intentionally make friends with these people. If you can't think of anyone and you live in a large-ish population center, find the local Catholic diocese and set up a meeting with a nun. *Seriously.* They'll do that for you. If you don't want to do that, spend a season of life looking out for God to put wisdom people in your path—they will come, I promise. Then, once you discover one, take them to lunch! Remember, contemplation is a posture of living, not a series of practices.

Observance of the Seasons

The Intention: To be totally open to the presence and activity of God.

The Why: Creation tells of the glory of God![4] Just observing the seasons—assuming that you live in a climate with some differentiation in seasons—is a way of tuning into the pattern of all spiritual things: living, dying, rising; living, dying, rising; all the way home.

The What: If you live in a place that has some weather/climate differentiation of seasons, follow the lead of the season. Do the things that the natural world around you invites you to do. And don't do the things that the natural world around you does not invite you to do. Find a swimming hole in the summer and burrow under a blanket by the fire in winter. Clean out your closet in the spring and plant some vegetables in the fall. Sing Christmas carols in December and January and pilgrimage to family graves in May. And eat outside as often as you can in the summer. If you live in a place with no weather/climate differentiation in the seasons, find other ways that the community around you marks time and follow it. For example, whether you're in school or not, buy some books in the fall as you endeavor to learn something new. Observance of the seasons reminds us of God's diversity, of humanity's cyclical story, and it frees us from the drudgery of each day being just like the last.

Beads

The Intention: To be totally open to the presence and activity of God.

The Why: We need tangible, physical reminders of unseen, spiritual things. Beads, and practices like it, are ways of integrating body and spirit into an embodied spiritual discipline.

The What: Get a set of beads—maybe a bracelet or a necklace—something that you can easily touch throughout your day. The beads can go around your wrist or live in your pocket or purse. Or maybe the beads can stay in the cupholder in your car or on your favorite side table, where you drink your morning coffee. The beads can be explicitly spiritual beads, like a rosary, or simply a beaded bracelet from the craft store. You can find spiritual beads that have a very specific rubric that guides you through a certain prayer or meditation for each bead, following the same words or patterns each time that you touch them. Or, like me, you can buy a nondescript beaded bracelet and, as your finger rubs over each bead, you can name a different fruit of the spirit (love, joy, peace, patience, kindness, goodness, faithfulness, gentleness, and self-control). As my fingers pass over the beads and I recite the fruits of the spirit, I pay attention to which one seems the hardest at that moment. I stop and take that fruit of the spirit as my spiritual invitation for the next hour or so.

Subtraction

The Intention: To be totally open to the presence and activity of God.

The Why: Our lives are so overfull. Practicing living with less frees us from the tyranny of more. Living with less declutters our life so that we have more room for God and more room for others. *Less is truly more!*

The What: Eliminate one thing in your line of sight by giving it away. A mug, a book, a painting, a shirt, *anything!* Give it away, practicing God's free, grace-filled giving. And as you live with less, your mind, heart, body, and soul release the clutter that crowds out our divine awareness. If everything in our line of sight is always filled with clutter, what space have we made to savor the gift of the few things that are truly meaningful to us, and what opportunity will we have to notice something new? There is a reason why monks and nuns live in simple cells. Simplicity is a physical representation of an uncluttered soul. Simplicity allows us to focus on one thing at a time and reduce distraction. As the Shaker ballad "Simple Gifts" promises: "'Tis the gift to be simple, 'tis the gift to be free!"

These practices are not ends to themselves; they are signposts to a posture of living that is embodying of a contemplative ethos. Try these practices and develop your own. Always remember that any act can become a contemplative act and any person a contemplative person.

6

Attention and Intention

Many of my days follow a predictable script: I wake up at seven in the morning, take the dog outside, and play with him for a few minutes. Next, I get ready for work, and I arrive at my office by eight thirty. Immediately, I am pulled into emails and meetings and phone calls that last until five thirty or six, when I head home and think about what meal to make or order with Bradley and what show we'll watch on our couch before going to bed and waking up the next day to start the pattern again. Rinse and repeat. Like you, during these habitual patterns, I experience many moments of happiness and enjoyment—with my dog outside; with my coworkers, laughing in the office; or relaxing with Bradley at home—but I am moving mostly from episode to episode, responding in ways that I have responded in the past and daydreaming about future trips and outcomes.

The good news is that it doesn't take much for me to shift my perspective to contemplation, bringing attention and intention to my daily routine. If I commit myself to attentive presence and let go of the corrupted belief that I am the solo agent of my destiny, I can adapt my habitual rule for living into a contemplative rule for life. I can become a contemplative. But my journey—and your journey—requires daily attention and intention. And don't worry—intention does not involve another set of steps. The work of intention, like the work of attention, is about letting go. *Subtracting, not adding.* Bringing intention to the work of attentive presence and letting go merely provides a background for the "why."

At the trust company in Nashville where I work, we have recently started creating staff guidelines for various processes. As we capture each process, before we begin to outline a series of steps to follow, we intentionally work to capture the "why." Our hope is that through being explicit about our intent that following a particular process will result in a more efficient outcome, provide greater opportunity for work-life balance, or exceed clients' expectations, we are connecting more dots than we were before. Centering prayer without intention is a way of practicing attention and presence, but it essentially becomes meditation when practiced without an anchor toward being totally open to the presence of the Holy. And meditation is wonderful—we should all practice it! But the spiritual disciplines that can lead one toward a life of contemplation are grounded not only in attention but also in intention. Intention to be totally open to the presence and activity of God.

From a contemplative posture, the fifteen minutes I spend alone with my dog in the morning can be a chance to see the divine in him and celebrate the love we share. I can be fully present to him, and I can celebrate the presence of God in Henry, my three-year-old Corgi. From a contemplative posture, I can moderate what I eat for lunch as I intentionally think about how a simpler way of living and eating would be healthy for my body. I can look for the signs of God in each of my coworkers. I can let go of my ways of striving and relearn that the world is God's. Without changing one activity of my day, and without adding in one extra practice, I can begin to live from a contemplative posture. It's as easy as changing what captures your attention and adding some intention to the rhythms of your day. Through active presence, intention, and economy of living, we, like the desert mothers and fathers before us, can leave the world of constant cares (*even while living in it*) and discover a spiritual path that grows our souls, not our egos.

Let's look in detail at each of the four foundations for contemplative living that I named in the prior chapter. The work is not in understanding a complex new system of theology or practice that requires years of study but instead in reordering your attention and intention toward these four central pillars for the contemplative life.

1. Believe That God Is Everywhere in Everything

While I was pastoring Christ Church, I took my staff leaders on an annual fall retreat to plan and recalibrate for the coming year. One year early in my role at Christ Church, I took the team to the Monteagle Sunday School Assembly to spend a weekend at the Edgeworth Inn, a beautiful bed-and-breakfast on the grounds of one of our region's last Chautauquas. After settling into our rooms at the inn, we met in the parlor off the foyer. On the wall immediately to my left after entering the room hung a plaque with words in Latin, which in English read: "*Bidden or not bidden, God is present.*" After seeing that bronze plaque in Monteagle, I had a similar plaque engraved with those words, which I've hung beside the front door in all the homes in which I've lived. I need the daily reminder that whether I call on God or not, God is present to me. I need as many tokens as I can collect to help light the path of enlightenment for me to become aware of God's prominence in the story of my life whether I recognize God in any particular moment or not.

The statement from the Edgeworth Inn's plaque is fundamentally contemplative. Contemplative spiritual practices open us to an awareness that even when we are not active in our thoughts or feelings toward God, God is active in us. So, the first principle of contemplation is a commitment to a growing awareness of finding God everywhere in everything. Every moment has the potential for holiness, for surprise, for grace. Living as if bidden or not bidden, "God is present" is a fundamental contemplative posture.

Either God is everywhere, or God is nowhere. And God is either in everything or God is in nothing. Because God is inside of each one of us—every living created thing, from the birds of the air to the trees of the field—we never leave God's presence. Every person whom we meet has something of God in them, however hidden, even from themselves.

The beautiful truth that we can take from the Hebrew Bible's Genesis story is that God is the start of all things. God breathed all things into existence. All created things come from God, carry a part of God, and return to God. Every moment has the makings of a spiritual encounter. Because everything we do, everywhere we go, and everyone we meet has a seed of God that we can look for, recognize, and celebrate.

We become contemplatives as we simply order our attention and intention to look for signposts to God in each moment and each person. God is everywhere and God is in all things, which is a different thing than saying that God is the agent of all things or the orderer of all things. Much spiritual harm has been done through people believing that God was behind the hurricane or that God caused the cancer. I invite you to try a semantic distinction: *God is not behind the hurricane, but God is in the hurricane. God is not behind the cancer, but God is in the cancer.*

I don't have a simple, buttoned-up explanation for the suffering and trouble in our world. The Christian tradition offers us a companion, not an explanation, in our suffering. Jesus came to earth to show us a better way to live and to offer us an embodied companion to our suffering by himself suffering the worst things we can experience: betrayal, misunderstanding, and death. Because Jesus experienced these things, we can know that God is not apart from but is a part of all our circumstances. God is our cogriever. God is everywhere, in everything. Our constant companion. The presence that is as close as our breath. Even in our breathing, we make God's name—inhaling *Yah,* exhaling *Weh.*

When we open ourselves to the realization that God is everywhere in everything, we can see every moment transformed into a contemplative moment and every encounter into a contemplative experience. When you leave your home and walk outside, you can bring awareness to the grass and ground beneath your feet, which carry the living, the life force of God, and the air that comes into your body as God's gift of sustaining presence. The person or pet you interact with can become an image bearer of the Holy. You can move through your day with an expectation of surprise as you look for the signs of God's presence around every corner.

Seeing God in everything—which can radically change our lives—requires attention and intention. Attention to the present moment, discussed in depth in the next section, and an intention to become aware of God's presence and spirit everywhere in everything. If we can focus our attention and intention in a contemplative posture, we will wake up from the sleepwalking that has characterized most of our lives, moving from episode to episode, day to day, event to event—an *intention-less* march through life's moments.

2. Attend to the Present Moment.

The secret is out that focused attention on the present moment is a prerequisite for contemplation. Nearly every spiritual, religious, and self-help guru reminds us that we have only the present. Focused attention on the present is the pathway to increased peace and greater physical and mental well-being. To hear someone like me go on about how important presence in the moment is sounds like a script that we have heard so many times that we can skip it. *Yet we are still so bad at it—me maybe most of all!*

We have not graduated yet from the school of presence. We will spend a lifetime learning how to train our minds to be present—present to the thing we are doing; present to the person we are encountering; and present to the bodily feelings we are experiencing.

When I was pastoring, I was part of an informal clergypersons book club. One season we read a little book on Benedictine spirituality by Wil Derkse called *The Rule of Benedict for Beginners*. Several months after we finished the book, one of the members of our group traveled to Europe and had an opportunity to visit with Derkse, who was living in the Netherlands as a philosophy professor and lay member of a religious community. My friend asked Derkse for the one piece of advice he might have for Christians living in America. Derkse quickly replied, "Sequential monotasking."

In our world of muchness and manyness, noise, crowds, and hurry, we have believed a lie that efficient multitasking is possible and preferable to sequential monotasking. But spiritual traditions remind us over and over to do one thing, do the thing fully, do the thing well, do the thing with your whole attention, and then move to the next thing. Brother Lawrence's classic book *The Practice of the Presence of God* tells the same truth as Brother Lawrence recounts the attentive presence he brings to washing each dish in the sink and how the dish washing became a contemplative practice for him.[1]

Spanish mystic St. Ignatius of Loyola, founder of the Jesuit community within the Roman Catholic Church, is credited with the Latin mantra "Age quod agis," which means: *Do what you are doing!* Jesuits today still carry St. Ignatius of Loyola's mantra daily in their hearts and minds as a constant reminder to focus on the present moment and to do the thing that they are doing.

Inner monologues of daydreams, worries, self-critique, or judgment fog so much of my action. On long car trips, many of us have the experience of getting to our destination and thinking, Where did the last thirty minutes or an hour go? We lost ourselves in our thoughts and can't remember how we got to the place where we were going. And we don't just escape our thoughts when we are driving. *We leave presence all the time.* We make our coffee thinking about the email that we just read and worrying about how to respond to it. We brush our daughter's hair in the morning, and we think about what we'll make for dinner eight hours later instead of feeling the softness of her ten-year-old hair as the comb slides through her mess of tangles. I have even finished a massage and thought, *Oh my goodness*, I have spent the last hour planning my activities for next week or rehearsing a drama with a coworker. *That was a waste of a hundred dollars!*

Be here now. Do what you are doing. These are truths that emerge from every major spiritual tradition. From self-help mindfulness teaching, Buddhist philosophy, and Christian dogma, the universal message comes through loud and clear: *attentive focus on the present moment is a necessary pillar to growing our souls and expanding our consciousness.* We must wake up from our sleepwalking. We must stop moving through life without attentive focus on the present. If we don't, our worries, our guilts, our fears, our envies, our judgments, and our self-critiques will constantly drag us down.

Time is an illusion. Spirituality reveals to us the mystery that time is eternal, without beginning or end. The way we mark time in seconds, minutes, and hours is helpful in our pursuit of efficient productivity and accomplishing of tasks, but marking of time in units of production is unhelpful in our awareness of our soul's connection to an eternal thread that connects us in the present to all that has been and all that will be. By connecting ourselves to the here and now, we connect ourselves to the eternal always. Now is all we have. Here is where we are. Everything else is an illusion.

All of us miss what is right in front of us because we're focused on the goals we are trying to reach, the fantasies of what might be, or the rehearsals of what went wrong. Not being present costs us so much joy and contentment. Either we're excited about something that might never happen, which can only lead to disappointment, or we're worried about a future outcome that hasn't even happened and may never happen, or we're stuck constantly replaying things that we have done to others and things others have done to us. All our worrying, fantasizing, and rehearsing keeps us from the beautiful gift of the moment right in front of us.

When we open ourselves to the present moment, we open ourselves to simple delight and to the full experience of pain—which is a gift as well because when we allow ourselves to experience pain, we lead ourselves toward the opportunity to process and move through pain. Attentive presence, even to suffering, is a kind of celebration because presence allows you to fully experience one moment so that the moment can have its journey in you, freeing you up to experience something different in the next moment rather than leaving an unresolved grief to reemerge at a later time.

One thing I have observed in some people as they age—and even in myself, though I am just now beginning my middle age—is that they have a lower tolerance for waiting. My beloved aunt Carol says that at her stage of life, if she has to stand in a line, Jesus better be at the end of it. My grandfather, Papaw as we called him, got to a place late in his life where he would rather hop in and out of the car, moving from restaurant to restaurant until he found an open table, rather than wait the twenty minutes that the first host told us we would need to wait before being seated.

The reason our capacity for waiting steadily declines as we age is because we are so well-practiced in not being present. With each year, we gain more experience escaping the present moment, which toward the end of life, for many of us, makes any experience that threatens to trap us in a moment of perceived boredom, waste, or dread intolerable.

With age comes wisdom and the fruition of the practiced habits we have spent a lifetime building. Babies and young children are the most present humans among us. They find delight in the simplest things. The unhindered laughter and joy that they experience from a simple smile, a funny joke, or a game is the sign that they are fully attentive to the present moment—to what is happening right in front of them. Our pets are the same. Without the self-consciousness of adolescents and adult humans, our pets are free to experience the present moment without a competing script of what happened before and what might happen next. As we age, our self-consciousness builds and our capacity for reasoning, intellect, and planning emerges. Because everything contains its opposite, the ability to process the past and plan for the future is a great gift, but hyperfocus on the past and future takes us further and further from the present.

When you are attentive to the present moment, even moments that you might perceive as boring, like waiting in an hour-long line for the Pirates of the Caribbean ride at Disney World, can become a pleasurable experience—or at least not a painful one. The pain of waiting comes from several iterations of nonpresence: a growing realization of everything you are missing and will not be able to get to; an invitation to think through a negative conversation that you had with your mother three days ago; or maybe a self-critique of a mistake you made last week.

What if while you are waiting you noticed the ground beneath your feet, the color of the person's hair in front of you, the feeling of being hot, cold, or just right? What if you took in the colors and textures of the stanchions separating you from the zigzagging lines of people beside you? *Easier said than done, right?!* I understand how unrealistic the expectation is that any of us would celebrate standing in a line with hundreds of people in front of us, but attentive presence to the people, sights, smells, and feelings of each moment will lead us toward greater joy.

Contemplation is presence. And presence is contemplation. When people ask me what separates a Christian contemplative practice from a Buddhist or mindfulness-based practice, I respond: "Not much at all." Attentive presence to the moment undergirds both contemplation and mindfulness. Everything is about sequential monotasking. The purpose is being here now and doing what you are doing. *The one difference between contemplation and mindfulness is the intention.* A Christian contemplative practice invokes an intention to—in the words of James Finley—be totally open to the presence and activity of God in the thing that you are doing or the person that you are experiencing.[2]

The best practice for attentive presence is the contemplative practice of centering prayer. Centering prayer, also known as contemplative prayer, is focused meditation with intention. A regular daily practice of centering prayer is the best preparation for a life of attentive presence.

Centering prayer, most clearly taught through the writings of Father Thomas Keating, involves sitting in a chair for twenty minutes (or less, as you are beginning) and letting go of all thoughts by attending to your breath or to a sacred word.[3] For twenty minutes, practitioners sit in stillness and empty their minds. Each time a thought pulls you back into the reprisals and plans of the mind, you either focus on your breathing—in and out, in and out—or return to a sacred word that you chose before the practice began as a way of returning you to your intention to empty your mind of thoughts.

The difference between centering prayer and meditation is simple—as you undertake centering prayer, in contrast to beginning a meditation practice, you form your intention to be totally open to the presence and activity of God. You undertake centering prayer from a posture of letting go, in recognition that God is always present, working, and rearranging you in spite of and in the absence of your work. Centering prayer balances all our doing with undoing and all our thinking with unthinking.

The point of centering prayer is not to get to a place of epiphany, when you still your mind and quiet your body enough to answer one of the looming existential questions that has haunted you. If the attractive thought that comes during your prayer sit is a revelation or answer to a burning question, *let it go*—returning to the breath or the sacred word—and trust that any true revelation of God will come back to you during your ordinary awareness.

Centering prayer is a practice of attentive presence. Emptying the mind, focusing on your breathing, being fully present to the bodily experience of sitting in a chair for twenty minutes, releasing your thoughts. The thoughts will come of course. Hundreds or even thousands of them in twenty minutes. In an often-repeated story about Father Thomas Keating's teaching of centering prayer, a nun lamented to him after her practice that she had had ten thousand thoughts during the twenty-minute sit. "How lovely," replied Father Thomas, continuing, "Ten thousand opportunities to return to God."[4]

Like exercise, twenty minutes of centering prayer builds new capacities within us to still our minds, focus on the present, and be attentive. We all need a centering prayer or meditation practice in our journey toward attentive presence. If you do not yet practice centering prayer, begin today. Begin with five minutes. Sit in a chair, set a timer, and focus on your breathing for five minutes, releasing every thought as the thoughts come.

The only way that you can get the practice of centering prayer wrong is to not do it or to get up before your timer goes off. Remember to think of your ten thousand interrupting thoughts as ten thousand opportunities to return to God through focus on your breath or the sacred word that reminds you of your intention to be totally open to the presence and activity of God. Feeling ashamed or embarrassed of how many times your mind wanders or how many thoughts emerge is just a deeper entry point to inattentive presence and the world of distraction, worry, and plans. As you have a thought, don't judge it; just release it by returning to your breath or to your sacred word.

Centering prayer is a practice of apophatic prayer, which is not a word that we use very often. First, let me explain its opposite—cataphatic prayer—which is prayer with a specific intent and focus. Intercessory prayer for others, prayers for ourselves, pleadings for favor and forgiveness are all examples of cataphatic prayer, a prayer that has particular focus toward something or someone. The prayer that involves us talking to God, telling God something, or asking God for something.

Apophatic prayer is the opposite of cataphatic prayer. Apophatic prayer is prayer that does not involve words, thoughts, or pleadings. Centering prayer is a form of apophatic prayer. The point of mentioning these two words is to remind us that we need everything in balance. Our life of prayer should include balance between cataphatic prayer and apophatic prayer. Most of us, however, are only used to cataphatic prayer and so our spiritual lives and our connections to the Holy are unbalanced. When we wonder why we don't have the insights or answers that we need, we should ask whether our diet of prayer includes apophatic prayer as well as cataphatic prayer. The long-term fruit of apophatic prayer is greater potential for attentive presence, which brings greater awareness of our bodies and what is happening right in front of us, right now.

Only in the present moment can we discover the answers to our questions and the solutions to our problems. A distracted mind that is stuck in the past or charging toward a potential future does not have any true or lasting answers to the big questions and problems that face us. Discernment happens in the present because good discernment requires us to notice and pay attention to what the presence of God inside of us is bearing witness to.

We plan from the mind, but we discern from the soul. And to discern from the soul requires us to be in touch with our souls, which can be rediscovered only through attentive engagement to the present moment. When we attentively engage with the present moment, our answers to how we are doing, what we want, how we are feeling, and what we really need are honest answers. Answers to those questions born from a place of rehearsals of the past or hopes for the future will only lead to us giving untrue answers to ourselves and to others.

Attentive presence is the pathway to discernment, peace, and joy. And attentive presence is a foundation for contemplation. The most impactful practice that we can undertake in our pursuit of attentive presence is a regular diet and practice of apophatic, or centering, prayer.

3. Acknowledge That the Work Is God's, not Ours

Contemplative spiritual practices are practices where the primary work or fruit from the practice is God's responsibility, not ours. Father Richard Rohr—in his book about contemplative spirituality, *The Naked Now*—talks about the disease of functional atheism that infects our churches. Functional atheism, according to Father Rohr, is the underlying belief that if anything good is going to happen, it's going to be because we did something. Unfortunately, functional atheism is rampant throughout the Christian Church.[5]

For six years, I had the privilege of serving as the executive pastor of Christ Church in Nashville. I loved my time there and woke up every day of those six years excited to go to work, but in truth, I'm still recovering from the quiet pain that those years caused me. Christ Church was a phenomenon. One of, if not the first, megachurches in the booming town of Nashville, Christ Church was a celebrity-studded congregation of country and gospel music superstars. Our choir was nominated for a Grammy Award and traveled the globe singing in a charismatic Black gospel style that was especially popular in Japan after the success of the *Sister Act* movie franchise.

In its heyday, the life of the church was vibrant, fun, and carried the airs of self-proclaimed significance. I came to the church during its golden age. Wynonna Judd serenaded us on Christmas Eve; on Easter Sunday, I fought for a parking spot and seat in the crammed-full large auditorium. And while I had been a part of the church during its arc of numerical growth, I was invited to serve as pastor during the transition after the church's founding pastor, who served for fifty-four years, had left; after the global economic crisis in 2008; and during a time when the neighborhoods of Nashville were changing and wealthy suburban families were moving out of the city limits into suburbs that had once been considered rural.

When I accepted the position in the fall of 2013, Sunday morning attendance averages had dropped from over four thousand to just under two thousand, and annual giving had similarly halved. The neighborhood around the church, which had once been suburban and mostly white, was now the home to the largest Kurdish population in the world outside of the Middle East. Musical tastes within church music had changed and green-robed choirs of white people singing music born from the Black church were no longer in fashion. The red-and-green paisley custom carpet in the sanctuary screamed of its installation year (1988), and the remaining debt on the church's last building project still loomed in the eight-figure range.

What I didn't fully appreciate at the time, as a twenty-nine-year-old lawyer-turned-pastor, was that the church was hiring me in the hopes that an executive, business-minded person could figure out how to get the attendance numbers back up and return the church to its status as a national trendsetter and regional megachurch powerhouse. But 1991 was never coming again because 1991 was never coming again. Demographic shifts, neighborhood shifts, taste and style shifts, and overall national church engagement shifts meant that the "good ole days" were not coming again for Christ Church. And depending on whom you asked, the old days weren't all that good. Like all influential churches that make a big splash, Christ Church had its allotment of affairs, quiet scandals that church leaders needed to resolve quickly to protect the church's reputation, and a complex history over the theology of human sexuality and the honoring of different ethnic communities.

And there was so much good in Christ Church's past as well. A beloved founding pastor and his saintly wife and the birth of ministries and businesses, including the popular Dave Ramsey Financial Peace empire. *Both-and.* The wheat grows alongside the chaff. None of our lives and none of our churches are immune from the complex and competing histories of benevolent institutions and money-making empires all within the same story.

For every day of the six years that I led Christ Church, I went to work knowing that the unspoken—and a few times, spoken—expectation for my role was to find the rabbit to pull out of the hat to bring the people back, build up the church coffers, get the debt paid off, and restore our status as a church of prominence. And my story is not unique; every pastor of a church experiencing its second or third life after the great parades have passed by understands what I am describing.

During those six years, we did a lot of remarkable things and had a lot of fun along the way. The staff loved each other well and felt like family. The congregation grew in little ways, and (I hope) some people's lives were changed for the better. But at the end of my tenure, when the time became natural to transition the church to a new, younger generation of church leadership, the church was smaller than when I had started, giving had decreased even further, and there was still around seven million dollars of debt remaining from the church's last building project, from twenty years ago. Other work was now needed—new roofs, new mechanical units, and aesthetic updates.

I was so tired. Bodily tired. Mentally tired. Soul tired. I didn't really have the language for what I was experiencing. I had enjoyed pastoring Christ Church, but now that my tenure had finished, I had developed an allergy to evangelicalism and megachurches. I couldn't stand to go near any church or spiritual activity that seemed at all cool, relevant, trendy, or important. I healed in smaller spiritual communities and eventually joined a 150-year-old decidedly uncool Presbyterian church that welcomed the LGBTQ+ community and allowed me, for the first time in my life, to belong to a community where I could show up fully as a gay man.

I can now see the functional atheism at work in myself and in so many of the well-meaning members and leaders of Christ Church who believed that there was some strategy or program we could implement to reverse course from decline back to growth. And while we tried thing after thing, we were missing all of God's opportunities to learn from and grow out of the gift of a church in decline. I'm afraid that I missed a lot of the invitations to grow in humility, courage, faithfulness, perseverance, and justice that were offered to me during those years while I worked to turn the ship around. And because God is so good, these lessons are still coming around for me and I'm slowly picking some of them up.

Contemplative spirituality is about letting go and giving up control. It is about recognizing that any hard or important work is God's, not ours. The best we can do is discern where God is working and join God in that work.

Contemplative living offers the balance that our souls are hungry for after our lifetimes of striving, working, and planning on God's supposed behalf. Even those of us trying to live into an awareness that God is love and grace in its purest forms and that there is nothing that we can do to get God to love us more and nothing that we can do to get God to love us less still struggle with feeling like we are the principal agents in our relationship with God.

God is primarily responsible for your relationship with the Holy, but you are primarily responsible for growing your soul.

God created us into being. We are bearers of the image of God. God gives us the breath inside our lungs. Our goal in life, despite what many of us were taught, is not to claw our way back to God. God has always been holding us in being. We are always in God's presence.

"Where can I go from your Spirit? Where can I flee from your presence? If I go up to the heavens, you are there; If I make my bed in the depths, you are there. If I rise on the wings of the dawn, if I settle on the far side of the sea, even there your hand will guide me, your right hand will hold me fast" (Psalms 139:7–10 NIV).

God is pursuing you. God is holding you. God is keeping you. You are beloved by God, and you belong to God whether you acknowledge the gift or not. Contemplative spirituality puts the agency for relationship back into God's hands. God is the agent, doer, and giver; we are the receiver. Contemplative spiritual practices, like centering prayer, are ways for us to practice letting go and not doing, all in recognition of the distinction in responsibility between God and us.

If we are doing and holding tight, we are the agents of our own relationship with God. We must give up our quest to get to God. When we let go is when we will finally realize that God has held us all along. When we finally cease all our strivings, we will finally be able to discover that God has always been with us—not because of how hard we have worked but because God's essential nature is to be in community with God's beloved creation.

Responsibility for our souls is another matter. Our souls are our receptors for God. God is always with us, and God is within each one of us, but our capacity to recognize and tap into God's eternal, unchanging presence lies within the condition of our souls. Our souls, also described as our spirits, are the truest part of ourselves. The virtues that are the Enneagram's reflection of our true selves are part of our souls. Our souls are the part of us that is eternal and that death cannot kill.

"And the dust returns to the ground it came from, and the spirit returns to God who gave it" (Ecclesiastes 12:7, NIV).

We all have a soul, or a spirit, but whether our soul is well fed or malnourished is our doing. Even the vilest of people who are least interested in the things of the spirit have a soul buried within that is waiting to be awakened by something that is true, beautiful, or good.

The spiritual practices that we embrace—whether fasting, fixed hour of prayer, centering prayer, walking a labyrinth, or putting together a jigsaw puzzle with intention—are all ways of growing our souls. As our souls grow, our awareness of our virtues turns up and our dependence on our passions—which have always just been the strategies that we adopted to face the world's challenges—turns down.

Contemplation is the pathway to growing our souls. Contemplative spiritual practices are the gifts that we give our souls. Our lifetime of work is to attend to growing our soul. To feed our souls and starve our egos. Lean into our virtues and turn away from our passions.

Just as we do not have to go get our virtues but instead rediscover them within us, soul work is the same. You have a soul. *Period.* Because you are made by God, for God, and held together in God. Our work is not to create a soul but to grow what is already there.

So much of the so-called spiritual work that we do is in service of our egos, not our souls. When I, in all my Enneagram 2-ness, help somebody as a strategy to securing place and belonging in their life or altruistic status in the eyes of someone watching, I have not grown my soul; I have fed my ego and my passion. Remember that our passions, and the Enneagram personalities that they inform, are not bad or evil. If I help somebody and get recognition for it, great. Hopefully, the person is better off, and I've gotten my ego fix for the day. It's okay. God is still God and I'm still God's beloved creation! But my soul hasn't expanded.

If during my years pastoring at Christ Church I had had the success we all were hoping for—doubled the congregation's size, returned giving levels to 2007 numbers, and rebuilt our reputation across our city—the success would have been fine, but the achievement would have been for ourselves, not for God and not for our souls. As long as we are measuring, counting, and accumulating, we are feeding our personalities. But when we let go of outcomes, when we trust God to do the work, when we act from a place of humility rather than pride, serenity rather than anger, truthfulness rather than deceit, equanimity rather than envy, nonattachment rather than greed, courage rather than fear, sobriety rather than gluttony, innocence rather than lust, and action rather than sloth, our souls expand and our awareness of God and our capacity to enjoy the benefits of unitive relationship with the Holy will grow.

Trust the work to God and focus on growing your soul through contemplation.

Contemplation is the key to soul growth because contemplation is inherently unproductive in the world's eyes. We must leave the world's economy of wins and losses to find our way to the economy of God. Contemplative spiritual practices don't bring results in measurable ways, and they are not particularly noteworthy in the eyes of anyone else.

What have you accomplished through centering prayer? Who cares that you walked the labyrinth? The unproductive, unimpressive contemplative practices are the ones that have the greatest effect on our soul's growth.

Fasting is a traditional contemplative practice across a range of religious traditions, including Christianity. But for fasting to be an act of contemplation, fasting must be private. In the words of Jesus, "When you fast, do not look somber as the hypocrites do, for they disfigure their faces to show others they are fasting. Truly I tell you, they have received their reward in full. But when you fast, put oil on your head and wash your face, so that it will not be obvious to others that you are fasting, but only to your Father, who is unseen; and your Father, who sees what is done in secret, will reward you" (Matthew 6:16–18 NIV).

My suggestion is that the reward of the Father in Jesus's lesson to his followers is not any salvific or status-bearing reward—remember we already all come from God, belong to God, and return to God—but an enhanced receptor to the delights of God. *A soul that is growing and expanding.* As our ego diminishes and our soul expands, we grow in joy, peace, contentment, and all enlightened things "on earth as it is in heaven."

The reward of contemplation is soul growth. And soul growth is not measurable or enviable. Soul growth is personal. Soul growth is our responsibility. It is the thing in the spiritual life that is ours to do, but evolution doesn't happen through active or works-oriented spirituality. Soul growth happens only through contemplation.

The fact that you are reading or listening to this book means that you are interested in soul growth and have undoubtedly engaged with practices throughout your lifetime that have expanded your soul's receptivity to the things of God. You were a contemplative before you even had the word!

Any time that you have recognized God somewhere unexpected; any time that you have attentively engaged with the present moment; any time that you have ceased your striving and released the work and its outcomes to God; and any time that you have engaged in simplicity of lifestyle as a way to declutter your life and make room for God, you have been engaged in contemplative living. I don't care if you ever embrace the words of the Enneagram or the words that I offer for contemplative spirituality. *The words don't matter.* The underlying concepts are what matter. Plenty of people have done the work that the Enneagram invites, of moving from passion to virtue without ever having heard of the system. And plenty of people from all types of religious and spiritual traditions have seen their souls expand without ever adopting the language of contemplation. Anyone committed to the growth of their soul from a place of letting go, undoing, and opening has found their way to the contemplative journey.

4. Practice Simplicity in Living

The final bedrock for contemplation is simplicity in living. I like the succinct articulation of contemplation as cutting out a space for the divine because this description reminds us that the more space we make in our lives—in every way, from physical space to mental and emotional space—the more room is made for soul growth.

One of my favorite activities is decluttering. It is the Enneagram 1 wing in me, I guess, but I never feel better than after I have emptied and organized a drawer or given a pile of clothes away to Goodwill. I cannot explain why exactly, but I find great satisfaction in looking around me and seeing things in order—or seeing less of something than I saw a few minutes prior. Living with less is good for me.

The fundamental premise behind contemplation as compared to other ways of living is that contemplation takes on a posture of letting go and opening. The opposite of contemplation is taking on, accumulating, and trying harder. When we practice simplicity in our living—which is possible in many different areas of our lives—we posture ourselves toward that of a contemplative.

The desert mothers and fathers left the cities and towns they lived in because they felt that materialism and excess bulk were inhibitors to the spiritual life. They sought a context and surroundings that were simple and, in many cases, austere as a pathway to join the way of Jesus in his poverty, with the goal of freeing up more space to hear from God and grow their souls.

A personalized version of simplicity of living, tailored to our own callings and needs, is our invitation toward embracing the contemplative life. You don't have to renounce the world and move to a convent to live more simply. You can start by eating less, buying less, living with less. A decade ago, I fell in love with the lyric to a song by Point of Grace—a Christian recording group—that goes, "Have what you want and want what you have."[6] When I first heard the lyric, I thought of how quickly the things I used to want lose their luster. My home and closet are full of things that I just had to have and now don't even notice anymore.

Our excessive accumulations distract us from the meaning and beauty of the few things that we really enjoy. Environmental cues that carve out a space for divine and godly awareness support our contemplative path and its posture of letting go. Although we can live more simply in many areas of our lives, I want to focus on what I'll describe as the big four: noise, stuff, food, and technology. You will no doubt notice other ways in which you have bulked up your life in a manner that distracts from God, but I dare say that all of us struggle with these four.

Noise

We are rarely in the company of silence. The radio or engagement with our phones accompanies our alone time, even in cars and private spaces. We play music while we wash the dishes. We have the TV on while we fall asleep. Many of us work in offices or customer-oriented settings where we don't have the luxury of privacy or quiet when we want it.

Noise is an inhibitor to soul growth because it ensures that we always have something to think about, even when our thoughts may be under control. If there is spiritual value in the practice of centering prayer and emptying your mind of thoughts, then there is surely spiritual value to eliminating some of the noisy distractions in your external settings. Contemplation requires attention and intention.

Noise without purpose is a threat to both our attention and our intention because nonpurposeful noise crowds out faithful presence and distracts us from good discernment.

Think of ways you can eliminate unnecessary noise from your life. You can drive home from work a couple of days a week with the radio off and your phone on silent, paying attention to what you hear, what you see, what you sense deep within.

A regular practice of centering prayer—sitting in silence and stillness for twenty minutes—is an antidote to noise. Even our spiritual communities are not immune from the noise that keeps us from attention and intention. I've heard a pastor use the words "sonic violence" to describe the way in which many of our modern churches ensure that we never have a moment in worship when someone isn't talking or music isn't loudly playing.

Stuff

The stuff we accumulate is personal to us and each of us has things that we tend to hoard unnecessarily. All our stuff calls for our attention. The more attention we give to our stuff—to its maintenance, its protection, and its further accumulation—the less attention we have to give to our souls and to our spiritual journeys.

All cultures, eras of history, and religions tell the same story: the more we accumulate, the less happy we are. And as someone who likes expensive things, I am not trying to shame anyone from having nice things. I get it. *Truly.* I have some nice things and I would like to have some more nice things. But we all must be honest with ourselves about the ways in which our stuff has crowded out our souls. The more stuff we have, the more time needs to be devoted to its care, which takes time away from any attentive presence and soul work.

Think of the ways in which you might live with less. Living with less creates an uncluttered line of sight that allows the curated things you do keep to carry their full meaning, allowing you to appreciate them for the utility or joy they bring.

Food

Food isn't a trigger for all of us, but it is for enough of us to mention it here. Food, which can be substituted for alcohol, marijuana, or any of the substances we can ingest into our bodies as sources of distraction or pleasure, can be another way to crowd out the soul. Overindulgence in any form is a distraction from attentive presence, dulling our senses and abilities to focus on what's happening right now, right in front of us.

Our invitation is to pay attention to our numbing strategies and notice the ways in which we use them to escape being present in the moment. Then we should ask ourselves, What part of the present moment are we trying to escape? Sure, in times of intense pain, suffering, or grief, we turn to our well-practiced strategies of avoidance; in moderation, for a time, those escapes can feel helpful. But if I am honest, most of my numbing strategies are the result of boredom.

Contemplative spiritual practices build our muscles to be able to enjoy moments and experiences that are ordinary, without having to make them extraordinary in some way. Any chance that we have to be content with less (of anything) is a practice in contemplation.

Technology

Not much needs to be said about the ways in which our growing addiction to technology in all its forms is crowding out the growth of our souls. We all know it, yet it is so hard to avoid. We have the greatest invention ever created presenting endless opportunities for distraction from the present moment right in our pockets—or in our hands, more likely!

Wiser people than me have written and will continue to write about the ways in which we need to review and edit our habits around technology, but here we should remember that technology has the potential to stunt a growing contemplative life.

I hope that what you are beginning to see is that the pathway to becoming a contemplative is no great secret. We are on the contemplative journey when we orient toward

finding God everywhere in everything;
focusing in on the present;
trusting God to the work; and
pursuing simplicity in living.

All contemplative spiritual practices—of which there are an infinite number because any activity can become a contemplative practice with the right intention brought to it—rest on these principles. We can all become contemplatives, even in our modern lives of family, work, and play. But don't be fooled by the simplicity that contemplation offers: if we don't bring awareness and intention to the ways in which we move through our days, we will miss the contemplative opportunities right in front of us. Attention and intention are the fundamental building blocks for contemplative living.

If you were expecting a checklist of specific practices that would be exactly right for each Enneagram type, I apologize. We all need centering prayer—every single one of us. It's the fundamental contemplative practice that invites each Enneagram type to a lifetime of practice, of falling down and getting back up again. And in our early days and years of exploring contemplation, we all need to try the well-traveled practices that are traditional to the contemplative life. All three of the Abrahamic traditions—Judaism, Christianity, and Islam—include seven practices: fixed hour of prayer, Sabbath keeping, fasting, almsgiving, sacred meal, observance of the seasons, and pilgrimage. Practicing centering prayer and these traditional seven will be good for all of us. And as we practice them, we'll learn the attention and intention behind contemplative spiritual practices, which then allows us to discover our own.

Again, as James Finley reminds us, "any act, habitually entered into with your whole heart, as a way of awakening, deepening, and sustaining a contemplative experience of the inherent holiness of the present moment" can become your contemplative practice.[7] Your Enneagram number does not have any practices that belong to it alone. Take on the practice of centering prayer as your commitment, explore the other classical contemplative practices, and then develop your own practice!

What are you waiting for?

7

Linking the Tools Together

When the virtue inside each one of us—hidden for so long—finally reemerges on the surface, our virtue represents the purest part of us. The virtue is unbruised by all our life's experiences because it has been hidden away.

When Enneagram 8s finally get to innocence, their innocence is purer and freer than the innocence that the rest of us experience. The same is true for every number. When 1s finally reclaim the precious virtue of serenity, they can experience the purest serenity that the world can offer. When Enneagram 2s finally accept their mantle of humility, they have the potential to express a humility that is deeper and more honest than the humility available to every other Enneagram type. Enneagram 3s have the greatest ability to follow their own personal North Star as far as it will lead them into a full expression of their identity and calling. And Enneagram 4s have the highest capacity for right-sized, balanced emotions than any other number.

The beautiful mystery hiding within the wisdom of the Enneagram virtues and passions is that the thing that is truest about you is, in so many ways, the thing you have most forgotten. Enneagram 5s are capable of the greatest openhearted nonattachment, and Enneagram 6s can brave their deepest fears with the most dazzling and abiding hope. Enneagram 7s can find more meaning and joy in the sober, mundane moments of life than the rest of us could ever dream of finding. The gospel message—or the good news of the Enneagram—is that what feels the furthest off is deepest within. Taking right action is costly, but as Enneagram 9s can testify, it is even costlier not to take it.

And so, the story begins in virtue. Good news comes before the bad. Blessing comes before cursing. The virtues are hidden within us from the very beginning. They are the eternal part of us, connected to all people and all times. They are the gifts within us that never die. And the language of the Enneagram offers each of us one virtue most connected to our personalities that developed from the sacred mixing of nature and nurture, that is most particularly ours and is the gateway to the hidden room of virtue planted within us. Our lifetime of work—spiritually speaking—is to find our way through the muck and mud of our personalities, our passions, our fears, and our emotions, to rediscover and draw back into the light the storehouse of virtue inside.

We begin life as image bearers of God, each carrying a true self, reflected by the virtue attached to our Enneagram type. Our souls are expansive with a strong capacity for attentive presence, unbridled joy, and deep, passionate feeling.

We start adapting to the world around us, reacting to family and strangers alike. Giving them what we perceive they expect from us or reacting in defiance to their expectations—all in ways that are not true to who we are but are reflections of the adaptations that we have made. We quickly learn to protect our truest selves because we recognize they are vulnerable in the face of the world's rejection, apathy, or displeasure at our intrinsic ways of being.

Our personality grows. And as Enneagram students, we can name some things about these personalities through the nine Enneagram types. We become better and better at making these adaptations, and our personalities become so practiced that before too long, we have forgotten that we adapted at all.

We begin to believe that we are how we present ourselves to the world. We believe the lie that we are our Enneagram type. The world continues to reward us for acting in consistency with how the world has come to know and label us; and so, we adopt the label ourselves.

"I'm just a perfectionist, or a helper," we say. "I can't help that I speak my mind, and if you can't keep up, just let me finish on my own."

The world and, sadly, *we* fully believe that we are merely the personalities that our Enneagram types describe.

Somewhere along the way we (hopefully) notice that our personalities don't work for us as well as they used to. Sure, we've perfected them, and they help us navigate relationships and work. But we become tired of the ways in which our habitual patterns of responding and behaving keep giving us the same outcomes. We get tired of the trouble that we cause for ourselves. We're ready for something different. And so, we turn to self-help systems and faith-based practices. We work on ourselves and we find some success. But our success only lasts for so long. We need help after help, step after step, and cure after cure. After we have found that all our solutions and strivings have been in vain, we are finally ready to give up and resign ourselves to the *this-is-just-who-I-am* philosophy.

The Enneagram and contemplation do not have much to offer people who have not yet grown tired of themselves and their patterned, habitual responses. If people are still impressed with themselves and see themselves as the spiritual agents who are climbing God's hill that always leads upward, the reflective tools of the Enneagram and contemplation will seem unimportant and uninteresting. The Enneagram doesn't offer anything to someone who is happy with their strategies for finding love and belonging. And contemplation doesn't have anything to offer to anyone who feels like they can do lots of big things for God through their own efforts alone. *And bless those people! I'm not trying to save them.* But if you are like me and you have finally wearied of your patterned responses, and your soul feels starved even after you've climbed the hill, saved the people, and done "great things" for God, now you're ready! *The good stuff is coming next.*

When we finally reach the end of our devices, we're primed for a new way of seeing and a new way of being. We're now ready for a contemplative spiritual practice. We are ready to let go.

As you embark on your contemplative journey—which takes a lifetime and in which we are always, as St. Benedict reminds us, beginners—you begin practicing the postures of seeing God everywhere in everything, practicing presence, letting go of taking charge over your life and the world around you, and practicing simplicity in your lifestyle. As these habits build, you begin to see that everything you do has the potential to be a contemplative practice. Every act can be a contemplative act, with the right attention and intention. Everything you undertake is an opportunity to open yourself to the inherent holiness of the present moment.

The traditional contemplative practices, such as centering prayer, labyrinth walking, fasting, fixed hour of prayer, and the like, are beginning points to get you into the habit of contemplation. But after a time, you develop your own contemplative spiritual practices.

The fruit—which is not measurable or countable—of your commitment to contemplative spiritual practices and carrying a posture of contemplation throughout your hectic life is that your soul expands, ever so gradually. Your soul becomes larger. And the way you know your soul is growing is because your capacity for expressing and experiencing the fruits of the Holy Spirit that St. Paul offers us in 1 Galatians 5—love, joy, peace, patience, kindness, goodness, faithfulness, gentleness, and self-control—grows. You are more patient than you used to be. You are gentler than you used to be. You are more loving than you used to be.

As your soul expands—as evidenced through your growing awareness and expression of the fruits of the Spirit—your true self, which is the soul's reflection of the God image that you bear, begins to shine again. Suddenly, the truest part of you—expressed through your Enneagram virtue—becomes primary and your false self—expressed through your Enneagram passion—becomes secondary. The false self is always there and will wax and wane, but our spiritual progress becomes evident when we, and those around us, can acknowledge and notice the true self back in action. The true self that was always there but had been buried (or protected) under layers of adaptations and projections from the bulk of personality that built and grew in response to your perception of what the world wanted from you.

A process of letting go, animated by contemplation, has the potential to lead us on a journey from true self to false self and back to true self.

The reason I described this process in such a wandering way is to emphasize that it is a process and not a series of steps to take. The process is something that is done to you, more than something that you do. Your biggest contribution is finally getting to the point when you are sick enough of your habitual, misaligned strategies that you finally give up your quest of fighting, pushing, grabbing, measuring, and counting. Your part is small, and God's part is big.

Only when we come to the end of ourselves can we find God. Rising comes after dying, but dying comes first. Dying to false self, dying to Enneagram number, dying to personality, dying to our strategies. When we finally accept the defeat of a million deaths to our ego, our accomplishments, our protections, and our projections, we are ready to begin. *We are ready to grow!*

The spiritual life has no clear steps, and the process is not linear. The journey involves falling down and getting back up again, all the way home. We do right some days and we do wrong other days. But hopefully, as the proverb reveals, "The path of the righteous is like the morning sun, shining ever brighter till the full light of day" (Proverbs 4:18 NIV). Month after month. Year after year.

Suffering and loss are our greatest teachers. And when we respond to suffering and loss with willingness rather than willfulness, we allow them to have their journey in us, which naturally builds character, endurance, and hope. From false self to true self. Passion back to virtue.

The good news—or dare I say, *the gospel*—of the Enneagram is that the ways in which you have come to know yourself and the ways in which you have come to be known by others is the exact opposite of what is truest about you. You are not stuck in your Enneagram number. You can find the way out of your box!

And the pathway for transformation is letting go—the journey of contemplation. The hardest part of which is accepting that our growth is more about what God does in us than what we do for God. Our work is to declutter a space for the divine so that our souls can expand.

When I meet people who are far along the wisdom journey, whether that be through embracing the Enneagram and contemplative spirituality or other wisdom tools (remember, I am agnostic about the tools you use; it's just that the Enneagram and contemplation are mine to deliver), they often see more of themselves in the high, or healthy, side of all of the Enneagram numbers. Often, wisdom people of any age describe how they can recognize their Enneagram type more easily by recollecting their prior selves in seasons of life when they were not as engaged with or committed to growing their soul. But now, in later seasons of life, they tell me that they find resonance with descriptions of each number's healthiest iterations.

I am not surprised to hear wisdom people describe the evolution and soul growth that they see in themselves. As we grow in wisdom, we recapture the virtue of the true self that is most particular to our Enneagram type—serenity for 1s, humility for 2s, truthfulness for 3s, equanimity for 4s, nonattachment for 5s, courage for 6s, sobriety for 7s, innocence for 8s, and action for 9s. This expansion becomes the doorway into the room of virtue where all nine virtues live, not only the one aligned with your Enneagram type. Entering the room of virtue for your type opens the way into the room filled with all the other eight virtues and everything else that can be described as true, beautiful, and good.

Each virtue belongs most particularly to the Enneagram type with which the virtue is associated and describes the true self and the God image that each of us carries. Truth, beauty, and goodness are not just one thing; they are many—even infinite—things. Once we find our way into the room of virtue, we have access to everything true, beautiful, and good. When you meet someone who truly bears out the virtue of humility, you can easily identify other virtues, such as serenity, innocence, action, or courage in their lives. Similarly, when you meet a person who embodies courage, they will also demonstrate a sobriety of action and mind, dedication to truthfulness, and an equanimity in their emotions. Virtue leads to virtue.

Anyone who resists the Enneagram because of a limited idea that alignment with one Enneagram type constricts us does not understand the beautiful truth that as we find our way back to our true selves and our souls expand, the virtue that brought us there—our feature virtue—ushers us into the room of virtue that includes access for us to bear out anything and everything that is true, beautiful, and good.

The most evolved wisdom people among us are the least rigidly described. They are capable of surprising themselves and others. They can encounter unfamiliar places, new experiences, new people, and innovative ideas openly and nondefensively. They often surprise us by holding uncomfortable opinions or competing ideas in tension. They are the people who are most truly themselves yet are capable of adapting, flexing, changing, and evolving. They are anything but stuck.

And so, those of us who have committed to tools like the Enneagram and contemplation often find that over time, our personalities become less predictable as the hold that personality has over us lessens and the flourishing of the soul and its virtues expands. The healthiest and highest expression of each Enneagram type includes all nine virtues, not just one.

8

One Step Further

Into the Flow

Labyrinths have always intrigued me. When you follow the winding path of a labyrinth, you will eventually reach the center, no matter how many turns and switchbacks you make. The significance of walking a labyrinth is a mystery that signifies the spiritual journey, and even if you do nothing more than walk the labyrinth in silence, you have "done it right."

A labyrinth is different from a maze; while a maze can be malevolent, a labyrinth is always benevolent. The labyrinth's path guides the way to the center. You can't take a wrong turn. Labyrinths are helpful symbols for the spiritual life because they mirror the path of grace in which the

Holy leads us on a journey to the center. The spiritual life is always moving toward and directed by God, even when we feel deep in the weeds and caught in the hedges.

Labyrinths also remind us that our spiritual journey is connected to the spiritual journeys of everyone else known and unknown to us—living and dead. The center does not just belong to me or you. The center belongs to us. My stops and starts, and your stalls and stucks, are interwoven into the tapestry of life's beautiful and terrible adventure of living, dying, and rising, living, dying, and rising, all the way home.

As you look at the Enneagram diagram, notice the lines with arrows running between the numbers. The Enneagram

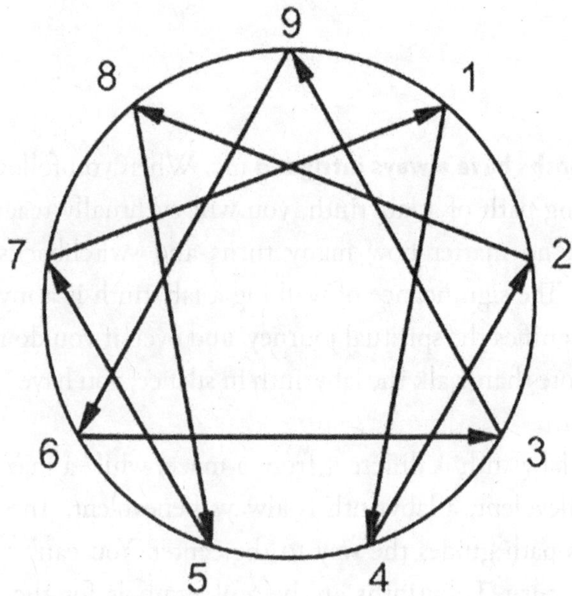

Figure 2. The Enneagram.[1]

is a labyrinth because each type connects to every other type through a visible web of connections illustrated by these lines. In Enneagram seminars, we often talk about these lines as the direction we move in during moments of stress and security. Enneagram 1s, for example, have a line with an arrow moving away from them and connecting them with Enneagram 4s. The line between 1s and 4s represents the movement toward the behaviors and actions of Enneagram 4s that Enneagram 1s can make when they are stressed. Enneagram 1s don't become Enneagram 4s. The primary passion for 1s remains anger and the primary virtue remains serenity. The wounding message in childhood that describes the motivating forces driving 1s to act is still the same: *you should be able to be perfect, and you shouldn't make mistakes, and you will only find love and belonging in the world if your behavior meets the mark.*

But the wisdom of the Enneagram teaches us that when Enneagram 1s are stressed, and they stay—either through their own choosing or through the strength of their circumstance—in stress long enough, the labyrinthine nature of the Enneagram will automatically lead them toward the position of the Enneagram 4 and the behaviors and actions that are available to Enneagram 4s. In the journey toward 4, from a healthy place, Enneagram 1s can embrace the nonduality of both-and thinking, but in the same movement, from an unhealthy place, Enneagram 1s can embrace behaviors of martyring victimhood.

Sticking with our example of the Enneagram 1, when 1s are in a secure place—which means that they are in a comfortable, routine, or known head, body, and heart space—they have access to the behaviors and actions of the Enneagram 7. So, 1s, in healthy secure spaces, can access the spontaneous freedom of the Enneagram 7 but, in unhealthy secure spaces, can access the unsatisfied energy of starting a million projects but never finishing one.

In my example of the movement that Enneagram 1s can make in stress and in security, I want you to notice two things. One is that the journey gives access to both healthy and unhealthy behaviors from the other Enneagram types, and stress does not automatically mean that you are accessing unhealthy behaviors in the same way that security does not automatically mean that you are accessing healthy ones. The second thing to notice in my explanation of movement for Enneagram 1s is that they retain their primary core motivations, their wounding message remains their wounding message, their primary passion remains their primary passion, and their primary virtue remains their primary virtue. However, the lines connecting the numbers give each number access to things that it needs but wouldn't naturally have access to within the bounds of its core number.

The Enneagram leads us to what we need when we need it, expanding our possibilities and helping us to reach beyond the predictable, patterned responses core to our established personalities. The lines between the Enneagram numbers represent a labyrinth between the numbers—a journey that we undertake each day, whether recognized or not.

If the Enneagram were a maze, and not a labyrinth, it would not be a tool for transformation and this book could not bear the title *Letting Go, Finding You*. Instead, we would have to learn a series of steps and practices to guide us toward the challenging work of accessing the healthiest attributes of our core Enneagram type and the attributes that we need from the other eight types that are not as natural. But the grace of the Enneagram offers us the flowing, ongoing movement of a labyrinth rather than the dead-ending frustrations of a maze.

As an Enneagram 2, I can look back on my life and see how, long before I knew the words or wisdom of the Enneagram, I was drawing on attributes most common to type 8 when I was stressed (in ways that both helped me and hurt me) and on attributes most common to type 4 when I was secure. I didn't need the language of the Enneagram to naturally make these moves, but once I had it, I could undertake these moves with attention and intention. Now, I can observe myself in stress and ask myself whether the core traits for type 8 can offer me anything helpful. Now, I can observe myself in secure places and ask myself whether the core traits for the Enneagram 4 can offer me, as an Enneagram 2, anything helpful and good.

This book is not specifically about movement and the Enneagram; it's about the beautiful intersection of the Enneagram and contemplation, which has the power to move us from passion and false self back toward virtue and true self. But the reason for this chapter's brief diversion is to underscore and make sense of the labyrinthine nature of the Enneagram that connects us to all the passions and all the virtues.

If you follow the movement that the lines between the numbers represent, you will find that the connections between Enneagram types reflected in the connections to wings (the numbers on each side of each number), as well as the arrows and lines representing the stress and security movements, connect every number to every other number. For example, 1s are connected through their wings of 9 and 2 and their movement in stress to 4 and in security to 7 to every other number on the Enneagram. If you pull out the figure, you will notice its labyrinth of movement and the ways in which each number is somehow—through wings and movement—connected to every other Enneagram type.

The revealing of connections between the Enneagram numbers underscores that when we find our way back to our core virtue and the true self that the virtue represents, we can access the virtues for all nine types. *We are in the flow.* We look both more like our true, idiosyncratic self and, at the same time, more like all the healthiest wisdom people who have ever lived, regardless of differences in our core Enneagram types. The life flow between numbers reveals dynamic, labyrinthine movement that leads us to all that we need, which, depending on the time and circumstance, is everything! Each of us needs, at some point, serenity, humility, truthfulness, equanimity, nonattachment, courage, sobriety, innocence, and action to grow our souls and fully bear out the Christ in us. And the Enneagram graciously offers us all that we need through a benevolent labyrinth of connections between the numbers.

However, when we stay stuck in our passions, the labyrinth becomes a maze as we move from dead end to dead end, passion to passion. Just as entrance to our feature virtue is the entry point or doorway into the room full of all the virtues, staying stuck in our passion leads us into the room of all the passions. The virtue reflected in our Enneagram number is the doorway into the room of virtues, and the passion reflected in our Enneagram number is the doorway into the room of passions.

When I'm stuck in the patterns of pride and the self-aggrandizing sense that I am here to fix and rescue everybody else while ignoring all the places where I need to be fixed and rescued, I don't have to look hard or long to find evidence of the passions of anger, deceit, envy, greed, fear, gluttony, lust, and sloth. When I become the martyring savior—pride in its fullest expression—I'm angry that other people don't help me as much as I help them; I'm self-deceiving because I ignore my true wants and instincts; I'm envious of how much easier everyone else's helper-free life seems; I'm greedy for friendships in my need for more and more affirmations to fill up my leaky cup; I'm fearful that everyone will leave me if they don't need me; I'm gluttonous in my pursuit of food and other numbing substances that can make me further forget about my own pressing needs; I'm lustful in my need for attention and affection; and I'm slothful in my commitment to identifying and meeting my own needs. Each of us can make our own set of connections to the ways in which our passion links us to the passions for all nine Enneagram types.

When we stay stuck in our passion, instead of the dynamic flow of movement that the Enneagram as labyrinth offers, we start to feel like the Enneagram is a never-ending maze of dead end after dead end. Each passion leads us deeper into the pit and further away from our true center. As we explore the room of passions, we get further from our true self, our false self expands, and our soul remains underdeveloped. The Enneagram stops feeling like a labyrinth that graciously guides us to all that we need and instead feels like a cruel trap that takes us further and further away from who God created us to be.

The secret is that whether the Enneagram is labyrinth or maze is up to us. We are the architects of our own journeys. Whether the Enneagram leads us to the flow of dynamic labyrinthine movement from false self to true self or to the frustrating stops and starts from passion to passion that buries our true selves with fresh layers of dirt every day is up to us.

We make the choice. The growth of our souls is in our own hands. But we find freedom as we let go. We have nothing more to try or to take on. We must let go to find ourselves. The Enneagram remains a labyrinth as we embrace a posture of contemplation through a lived experience of contemplative spiritual practices. But the Enneagram becomes a cruel maze, of our own making, through either willful indifference toward soul growth or the hellish road of "good" intentions to will ourselves to be good through a never-ending process of more steps, more "work," more striving, and more taking-on.

Letting go, finding you is the invitation of the Enneagram and contemplative spirituality. Each supports the other. As we let go of our quest to make ourselves good and instead submit ourselves to God's doing and to undergoing the offering of contemplative spirituality, we will find ourselves in the flow. The constant, dynamic flow of movement—from virtue to virtue. And our soul will continue to expand as the old strangleholds of personality fall away.

Does your life feel like a labyrinth, or does your life feel like a maze?

Do you feel like you are becoming freer, or do you feel like you are getting buried deeper and deeper?

Are your hands outstretched, palms up in the posture of letting go, or are your hands clenched up and withdrawn?

These are the honest analyses that the spiritual life invites us to make. These are the questions that we must consistently pause and ask ourselves. These are the testing grounds for whether our life is becoming more ruled by passions or by virtues. These are the questions that help us know whether our souls are expanding or restricting.

If, like me, you have felt like life has been a mixture of maze and labyrinth, but you want to do all you can do to allow the life flow of virtue to flow freely in you—a life flow that will make you feel connected to God and to every human who has lived—you must shift your perspective to one that is contemplative in nature.

We must open up, let go, allow God to do in us more than we could ever do for ourselves or for God. We must stop trying to strive our way to heaven or work our way out of hell. We must notice the inherent holiness in every present moment. We must find the reflection and evidence of God in everything. We must stop thinking in such dualistic, competitive, and mean-spirited ways, and we must open ourselves to the both-and, nondualistic awareness that two things can be true. We must shun partisanship and exclusionary thinking in every way. We must stop believing that the only way that we can cohere is by identifying a common enemy. We must allow new insights to deconstruct our old ways of thinking. *Letting go, finding you.*

We can't will our way to growth. Just as we can't make our way to God. We all belong to God because we have always all belonged to God. We all have a place at the table because a place was always set for us. Bidden or unbidden, God is present. Seen or unseen, virtue lives within you. Aware or unaware, we all reflect the image of God.

Will we be courageous enough to try something different? Will we stop forcing our way through the never-ending maze, or will we allow God to lead us through the labyrinth? If we will let go, open up, and allow God—through our embracing of contemplation rather than active, take-the-hill spirituality—we will, often imperceptibly, see passion and personality fall away while virtue and true self rise. And our souls will grow. And we will find deeper connection to the Holy, not because we did anything to make God connect with us more but because we let go of the things that had blocked us from awareness of our unbreakable connection to God.

We initially thought about titling this book *Let Go, Find You*, but I didn't like how imperative that title sounded. I wanted the tone to sound gentler, easier, kinder. I wanted you to see the transformation that this book invites as an undergoing and not an undertaking.

And so, we went with the gentler sounding *Letting Go, Finding You*. And through the subtle difference, I hope you understand that I have not meant to contribute any more spiritual teaching to the world that is harsh, tribal, or suggestive of some breach or disconnect between us and God.

But if you will allow me, I would like to call you—and call myself—into action, to say as clearly and forcefully as I know how: *Let go so that you can find yourself!*

As we let go of old patterns of responding and behaving; as we let go of the false promises that our passions offer to us; as we let go of the false notion that God is far off, disappointed, and waiting for us to find our way back to God; and as we stop trying to save ourselves through steps, penances, and good deeds . . . we will finally find ourselves. We will find our purpose. We will find our virtue. We will uncover and grow our souls.

"For you died to this life, and your real life is hidden with Christ in God" (Colossians 3:3 NLT).

The rewiring that comes through letting go will change everything about the motivations that drive your actions. The contemplative work I am inviting you to will not change your personality or Enneagram type. The best parts will be transformed, not lost. Because your behavior will no longer be principally motivated by your passion or false self; instead, your behavior can be born out of your virtue—the truest self. Can you imagine how much better I, as an Enneagram 2, can love and serve and give to others from a fundamental motivation of humility rather than pride? Can you imagine how much more long-lasting (and even eternal) career success an Enneagram 3 can have when they commit to live out the full truth of who they are? Can you imagine how much empathetic, loving concern can be shown by an Enneagram 4 who connects with your feelings from a place of balanced equanimity instead of a place of envy and comparison? Can you imagine how much more deep rest an Enneagram 9 can enjoy after the satisfaction of doing the things only they truly can and will do rather than being consumed with busy, distracted doing?

Our journey is not from passion to virtue but from passion *back* to virtue—the place where we really began.

Conclusion

Keep Going—Don't Turn Back

The apostle Paul, in his New Testament letter to the church in Rome, grieved his life's dilemma: "I do not understand what I do. For what I want to do I do not do, but what I hate I do" (Romans 7:15 NIV). The wisdom of the Enneagram answers Paul's angst. We do the things we don't mean to do when we act from passion. And we can do as we meant to do only when we act from virtue.

My hunch is that Paul, without the language of the Enneagram, intuited that his besetting passion often got the best of him by leading him toward patterns of behavior motivated by anger, pride, deceit, envy, greed, fear, gluttony, lust, or sloth. Paul (like me, and like you, too, if you have read this far), knew that there was a better way to live and a better way to be. He knew that a virtue hid somewhere beneath his passion. And furthermore, I suspect that Paul discovered that through commitment to a robust spiritual life, his virtue could break through the fence that his passion had built and—*in blessed moments*—shine through.

One of the greatest challenges to living from the place where our soul bears out its virtue, the divine in us, is that we fall in love with our projections. We have learned to rely on the things that seem to have always worked, only to relearn time and time again that they never worked all that well.

I heard from a person who recently had the opportunity to go on tour with a 1970s rock band that was known for their shocking outfits, extreme stage behavior, and ear-piercing volume. Forty years after their breakthrough stadium shows, they were on a reunion tour. Now in their seventies, the band members donned the old outfits, put on the old makeup, and sang the familiar songs. And the strategy worked. The same fans who had followed them in their youth came back to remember the energy that had captivated them forty years ago. Each band member enjoyed reentering the magic of an earlier era—albeit a few artificial hips ago—now romanticized and faded by years so that the challenges and indiscretions were mostly forgotten.

For the duration of the show, it almost seemed as if everyone was still as they once were, frozen in time. But after the show ended and the fans dispersed, the old rockers returned to their bus. Knees creaked as they climbed the bus stairs while pulling off their wigs and heading straight to the mirror to wipe off the makeup. Thirty minutes later, the band members were sitting on plush leather sofas in the front section of the bus, reading the *Wall Street Journal*, drinking coffee, and listening to Beethoven's Ninth Symphony on the Bose stereo.

In the forty years that had passed, the band members had become new people. Their tastes had changed; their looks had changed; and their spiritual lives had changed. Sure, they enjoyed putting on the clothes of an old life—but only for two hours. They aren't those people anymore.

The deep exploration of self and the Holy, offered through Enneagram wisdom and contemplation, calls us away from old patterns to discover that we have been made new. Our lives must be dynamic for us to become unstuck from Paul's trap of not doing the things we want to do and doing the things we hate. Sometimes, like the old rockers, we glimpse an old self in the mirror and smile, but if we return too long, we quickly realize that the clothes don't fit anymore.

Father Richard Rohr, in *Immortal Diamond*, writes that humans always have a tendency, when on the cusp of new growth, to turn back: "When you love, you die to self because you have awoken to a larger truth and it scares you and you want to retreat and enfold back to small self. Or you can expand and die to small self and open to something greater."[1]

I spent the first thirty years of my life pushing down the gnawing knowledge that I was gay, because I was sure that God didn't want me to be gay. In my early thirties, I accidentally discovered some of the writing and work of the emergent church movement from the 1990s. I read books by Phyllis Tickle, Brian McLaren, and Tony Jones. I began to discover a new way of thinking about the Christian story. A way that challenged my inherited beliefs about substitutionary atonement, last things, the Bible, human sexuality, and more. Once my theology evolved, I had a challenging time justifying my self-denial when I no longer believed the things that I used to believe about God's designs for human sexuality.

And then I met Bradley. I fell in love. After some months of exploring a relationship in its springtime, what had been exhilarating became terrifying as I wondered if I was ready to leave my thirty-year-old system of belief behind to venture in a new uncertain direction that diverged from nearly all I thought I knew to be true, safe, and wise. I had awoken to a larger truth, and the larger truth scared me enough to want to retreat to my small self. And I retreated for a time. The smaller self is familiar. The smaller self feels safe. And in many ways, the smaller self is safe—safe from everything except from the most threatening thing of all: a winter of life filled with regrets. Avoiding the pulls and tugs to return to our small self is part of our lifetime of work.

The Enneagram reveals our small self, described mostly in this book as the false self that is animated by our passion, by giving us language to describe the self that emerged early in life to protect our larger, or true, self that felt too vulnerable and precious to expose to battering from those we love and the world around us. So, we settled into a life of being the "moral one," the "helpful one," the "successful one," the "interesting one," the "insightful one," the "loyal one," the "fun one," the "tough one," or the "likable one." And those small selves worked for a while, but if we're honest, at some point they stopped working. Along the way, we realize that all the moral certitude, helpful giving, success seeking, culture refining, information gathering, worst-case-scenario planning, adventure seeking, boundary making, and peacekeeping have cost us a lot. These strategies have cost us our hearts and our souls and kept us locked into small self, keeping the divine in us at bay while overplaying the us-in-us.

As we reach the end of this journey together, I cannot overemphasize the temptation to return to small self and put away the work of transformation. A soul that is open to all its truest truths is capable of being abused, misunderstood, wounded, and ridiculed. Transformation often feels very costly. People have come to love you and know you by the features of your small self. The moment you stop following your old script, many of the people who love you the most will ask you what is wrong and when the old "you" will be coming back. The work of growing your soul by unveiling the virtue-driven divinity in you and managing the passion-driven false self takes a lifetime to complete and requires daily, and truly hourly, commitment to not pick back up the layers that you have allowed to fall away.

For six years, during my time at Christ Church and the incubation of my journey to discover the difference between my false self and my true self, I had the privilege to pastor alongside my friend Dan. He was Christ Church's senior pastor and he generously invited me to join him in ministry, to share his role by overseeing the staff and executive functions of the church. The years we spent together were six of the most challenging and rewarding years of my life. In many ways, Dan was my tour guide to learning the wise lesson that returning to small self comes at too great a cost once your eyes have been opened to the larger self that lives beneath.

Dan came to Christ Church in the 1980s as its associate pastor. He was young, charismatic, and incredibly smart. And he could sing the roof off—which was especially important to a church that became a musical trendsetter. For ten years, from 1984 to 1994, he served Christ Church and he fit its culture and theology like a hand in a glove.

Then, in 1994, Dan had the opportunity to go to Phoenix to pastor another large church, Valley Cathedral. He spent ten years at Valley Cathedral, but something happened to him in those years that complicated his life significantly. He encountered the limitations of the small self and the wonderful promise of a larger self. In short, Dan grew his soul during his years in Phoenix to such an extent that the limitations of his Enneagram type 4 personality and the small self it represented no longer worked like they used to.

At Valley Cathedral, Dan became an Anglican, studied to become a licensed professional counselor, exposed sexual abuse and trauma in the church's past, and experienced the kind of transformation that can come only from loss when his wife, Trish, suffered a devasting brain aneurysm. The old-time religion didn't work any longer for him. Questions about neuroscience, the human genome project, and the systemic racism affecting the Hopi people living in his community expanded his sense of the world and, in turn, his sense of self.

Dan got the invitation to return to Nashville to serve Christ Church as its senior pastor, succeeding a well-loved founder who had served for over fifty years. Dan accepted the invitation, and he and Trish—still recovering from her traumatic brain injury—drove their car east to resettle in Nashville, hoping that the new season among old friends would help them to heal physically and emotionally.

The problem with "coming home" is that people expect you to still be as you were when you left them. At first, all seemed great. Dan was still the charismatic, smart, gospel-singing preacher that people at Christ Church had loved so much a decade prior, but he had changed in a thousand subtle ways. His worldview, his theology, and most importantly, his sense of self had adapted and evolved as his journey of suffering had led him to grow his soul. Without yet knowing the language of the Enneagram, I was able to see that passion had fallen away and virtue had emerged and that Dan had become a man of wisdom, balance, and equanimity.

The sad truth is that lots of people did not like it. They wanted the old Dan back. They wanted the Dan of ten years ago to return. They were putting on Dan, through their criticisms, their own sense of loss and grief that an old way of living was slipping away as the exciting circus of mid-century Pentecostalism played its last card. But Dan had changed—just as the world had changed—and he had given up pieces of false self so that a truer self could rise, and there was no turning back.

You can't unsee what you've seen. Dan couldn't bring himself to regress to a decade-old version of himself, and he paid a great price for it. But fortunately for his soul, and for me who was watching, the price he paid was in friendships and position, not in the matters of soul and virtue. I learned a lot of great things from him, but the most important one was "to thine own [true] self be true." I'm happy to say that Dan is thriving in a new season of life as a counselor, spiritual director, and bishop.

I'm not sure that anyone comes to deep Enneagram work who is not in some version of deconstructing and reconstructing from lots of ways of being—from theology to worldview, to vocation and beyond. Employing the wisdom of the Enneagram to learn more about yourself than just your number calls into question old patterns, old beliefs, and old ways of being. And after a time of expansion in self-knowledge, the temptation always comes to turn back and return to what seems like an easier way of living. But remember, the false self never worked all that well for you. The false self helped you navigate early relationships and younger days, but always in ways that limited you rather than expanded you. Your Enneagram type is limiting. Your passion is limiting. Your true self, your soul, your virtue is limitless. Which will you serve?

Who do you now know yourself to be?

Can you embrace a change in how you see yourself and how you are known by others?

Will you give up the familiarity of the false self, characterized by your Enneagram number and passion, to—like Abram—get up, pick up your mat, and go in a new direction that will be revealed only step by step as you travel?

Letting go, finding you.
Let go, find you.
Let go.
Find.
You.

May it be so for you, and may it be so for me.

Thanksgivings

The contents and direction of this book have evolved through different iterations and starts guided by my Enneagram seminars, cohorts, and particularly, my students. But the current version in your hands, or in your ears, really began when I realized that I needed help. I'm a collaborator at heart—a consensus builder and a verbal processor. Anything good that I have created has always been a group effort. I needed an agent and publisher to help me make sense of my scattered ideas.

I'm a devoted follower of the Quaker impulse that "way will open, and way will close," and so, when I got an email unexpectedly one day from an agent named Estee Zandee at The Bindery, I paid attention. Estee and I began working together, and when she had the opportunity to move from the agency side of things to the publishing side of things, she linked me with The Bindery's managing director, Ingrid Beck, who is as responsible as I am for this book's birthing. Ingrid took lots of raw data and made beautiful sense of it all. I will be forever grateful for her faithful partnership in this endeavor.

As Ingrid began looking for publishers to further refine our work, Lisa Kloskin at Broadleaf Books was a fit right away. Lisa cheered me on and further reshaped *Letting Go, Finding You*, including leading us to its title. I am indebted to my village of experts, cheerleaders, and wisdom persons for their friendship, partnership, and hunger for soul growth.

And I hope you haven't tired of the hero worship of the Stabiles, but I wouldn't have the Enneagram without Suzanne and I wouldn't have contemplation without Joe. They have changed everything about my life.

And finally, Bradley offered nurturing and championing partnership during the incubation of this book, and Henry offered faithful four-legged companionship beneath my chair while I wrote each word.

And to you . . . the reader, you are my reason.

Many, many thanks.

Notes

Introduction

1 Virtutepetens, "Enneagram integration" (image), https://commons.wikimedia.org/wiki/File:Enneagram_integration.JPG.
2 Dottie Rambo, "The Unseen Hand," *The Dottie Rambo Songbook* (Nashville: John T. Benson Publishing, 1968).

Chapter 1: Why Five-Step Spirituality Is No Longer Working

1 Barbara Brown Taylor, *Leaving Church: A Memoir of Faith* (San Francisco: HarperOne, 2006), 75.

Chapter 2: The Goal Is Transformation, Not Change

1 T. S. Eliot, "Little Gidding," in *Four Quartets*, ed. Christopher Ricks (New York: Harcourt, 2001), 59.
2 Brian D. McLaren, *The Great Spiritual Migration: How the World's Largest Religion Is Seeking a Better Way to Be Christian* (Colorado Springs, CO: Convergent Books, 2016), 45.
3 Henri J. M. Nouwen, *In the Name of Jesus: Reflections on Christian Leadership* (New York: Crossroad Publishing, 1989), 30.

Chapter 3: True Self vs. False Self

1 Rick Hanson, *Hardwiring Happiness: The New Brain Science of Contentment, Calm, and Confidence* (New York: Harmony Books, 2013), 45.
2 Don Richard Riso and Russ Hudson, *The Wisdom of the Enneagram: The Complete Guide to Psychological and Spiritual Growth for the Nine Personality Types* (New York: Bantam Books, 1999), 125.
3 Thich Nhat Hanh, *How to Eat* (Berkeley, CA: Parallax Press, 2014), 22.

Chapter 4: Twisting the Truth

1 Frederick Buechner, *Beyond Words: Daily Readings in the ABC's of Faith* (New York: HarperCollins, 2004).
2 Riso and Hudson, *The Wisdom of the Enneagram*, 133.
3 Originally posted by the Facebook account The Vista Room ATL.

Chapter 5: Contemplative Spirituality as a Way of Life

1 James Finley, *The Contemplative Heart* (Notre Dame, IN: Sorin Books, 2000), 46–47, 48.

2 Thomas Moore, *Meditations: On the Monk Who Dwells in Daily Life* (New York: Harper Collins, 1994), 45.
3 Eugene H. Peterson, *Working the Angles: The Shape of Pastoral Integrity* (Grand Rapids, MI: Eerdmans, 1989), 123.
4 Psalm 19:1 NIV; Romans 1:20 NIV.

Chapter 6: Attention and Intention

1 Brother Lawrence, *The Practice of the Presence of God* (New Kensington, PA: Whitaker House, 1982), 35.
2 James Finley, *Merton's Palace of Nowhere* (Notre Dame, IN: Ave Maria Press, 1978), 62.
3 Thomas Keating, O.C.S.O., *The Foundations for Centering Prayer and the Christian Contemplative Life: Open Mind, Open Heart; Invitation to Love; The Mystery of Christ* (London: Bloomsbury Academic, 2002).
4 Thomas Keating, *Open Mind, Open Heart: The Contemplative Dimension of the Gospel* (London: Continuum, 2006), 56.
5 Richard Rohr, *The Naked Now: Learning to See as the Mystics See* (New York: Crossroad Publishing, 2009).
6 Point of Grace, "How You Live (Turn Up the Music)," by Cindy Morgan, track 3 on *How You Live,* Warner Chappell Music, 2007.
7 Finley, *The Contemplative Heart,* 46–47, 48.

Chapter 8: One Step Further

1 Virtutepetens, "Enneagram integration" (image), https://commons.wikimedia.org/wiki/File:Enneagram_integration.JPG.

Conclusion: Keep Going—Don't Turn Back

1 Richard Rohr, *Immortal Diamond: The Search for Our True Self* (San Francisco: Jossey-Bass, 2013), 123.